A THIRD OF A LIFE

A THIRD OF A LIFE

A Family's 25 Years in Foreign Service

By Margaret Winkler

June, 2014

authorHOUSE®

AuthorHouse™ LLC
1663 Liberty Drive
Bloomington, IN 47403
www.authorhouse.com
Phone: 1-800-839-8640

Published by AuthorHouse   06/19/2014

ISBN: 978-1-4969-1792-8 (sc)
ISBN: 978-1-4969-1591-7 (e)

Library of Congress Control Number: 2014910251

DEDICATION

For Gordo

You were here the whole time.

TABLE OF CONTENTS

Sting: ---

"Memory is a neural muscle and once you begin to stretch it, it grows to accommodate everything that has ever happened to you."

INTRODUCTION

I call this memoir "A Third of a Life" with the intention of sparing whoever reads it an account of my whole life from childhood to today. The first third was happy and productive most of the time, but of interest only to family, not at all remarkable. The last third – the present – is a little sad, a coda, a winding down. Perhaps inevitable.

But the middle third is replete with one story after another, stories I would like to hand to my children and friends to remember the funny, exciting, unusual, sometimes scary, totally memorable bits, I would like to have them in print just in case someone is interested or curious. I am writing this in the middle of my ninth decade with enough perspective to reflect on these times, these attitudes, grateful to have lived them and to be able to remember them.

These stories have been leaking out of my head for 50 years, with many people saying "You've got to write a book."

All right, now I have finally gotten the kick in the pants to get going.

These stories recount my family's life in three foreign countries: Ethiopia, Ghana, and Iran. I end in New Mexico, enchanted land of our retirement.

We came from an affluent suburb of a large city. City and village afforded culture: theatre, music, pretty sophisticated friends. It wasn't that there wasn't enough. But in retrospect it is clear that one type of people living essentially the same way of life made for a complacency seeping into our lives.

Staying there, staying put, would have wrapped me and my family in prosperous provincialism. When the opportunity came to leave the physical place behind, thanks to the adventurous and restless nature of my husband, we got the chance to look at life through very different windows.

So when John F. Kennedy made his "ask not" speech, we were galvanized to try to comply. My husband left his Public Relations business (partly dedicated to raising the per capita consumption of pickles, candy and ice cream) to apply to and join a government agency whose mission was to tell America's story abroad. We picked up three little boys from their comfortable existence to drop them into a new life on a new continent. We hoped they would be empowered to navigate the course of their lives with street guides and maps beyond their limited suburban environs. Friends of course thought we were crazy. Maybe so.

When Gordon was appointed to a position in the United States Information Agency he went to Washington for several months of training. We had no idea where we would be going. "Worldwide available" was the rule. One evening he phoned to ask me what I thought of Ethiopia. My answer: "Tell me where it is and I will think about it." What, essentially, would be our mission? The objective was, broadly, to tell America's story abroad. Not as propaganda, exactly, but by example, to teach English (huge demand), to bring cultural events such as movies, theatrical events, art exhibitions, trade shows. and more. Also to facilitate student exchange. America was pretty popular in those days, thousands of students were anxious to go to the states to soak up its atmosphere.

We were shortly devastated by the assassination of the President. The resolve to make this effort work became even stronger, we felt it a responsibility. By coincidence Gordon physically resembled Kennedy in many peoples' eyes. This seemed to give us a connection to people abroad in a way

Little did we know what we were getting into. To telegraph the ending, we embarked on 25 years of wonder, excitement, some but little regret, education beyond our dreams, and a life style we could not have envisioned. And I believe we contributed a lot more to the betterment of the world – certainly to the betterment of ourselves - than we ever would had we not tried.

This conversation took place sometime in September of 1963, outside of Chicago. The participants are He: Gordon, Daddy; Me: clearly Myself; Dickie: oldest son, age 11; Andy, age 9; Billy, age 6

ME: How are we going to tell the kids?

HE: Let's tell them what's going to happen, why, when, straight up. (Ed. Note: you can tell he is a newspaper reporter.)

ME: You guys, come up here (on the king size bed.) Daddy and I have something very important to tell you.

BILLY: Let me get my blanket.

HE: Mom and I have made a very big decision to move away. A long way. To a country called Ethiopia, in Africa. Not forever, but for a long time. Because we think it will be good for all of us to meet different people. It could be hard for you to leave school, your friends, but you'll

have new ones. Maybe we'll get some pets like
monkeys and dogs and horses.

ME: The couple of times when Dad and I have gone
        to different countries in Europe and Mexico,
        we really liked finding out how other people
        lived, talked, ate and dressed.

HE: There could be some tough times when you're
        unhappy. We'll know and we'll talk about it. But
        we think you will like the whole business as it
        goes along.

DICKIE: Daddy, are you going to have a job?

HE: I am going to work for Uncle Sam instead of
        the Pickle Council.

ANDY: Can we take the Gielows? (friends across the
        street)

ME: No sweetheart, this is just for our family. Just
        you guys and Daddy and me. We are going at
        the end of the year, at Christmas time. We will
        go from New York, to Paris, France for a few
        days. Then to Rome, Italy; after a couple of
        days there we'll fly to Athens, Greece. Several
        days later we will fly through Cairo, Egypt and
        Khartoum in the Sudan, to get to Addis Ababa,
        where we will be living.

DICKIE: Do I have to take my cello?

ANDY: Are we going to live in a house?

DICKIE: No. We will live in a tent, dummy.

HE: As soon as we get to Addis we will take you to the American School, which won't feel very different, except for different kids.

BILLY: What's Africa?

ME: Africa is a continent, just like America is. Ethiopia is a country on the east edge of Africa, just north of Kenya.

   Dickie, go get your globe, and show Billy where we're going.

   You can tell your friends at school any time you want. Maybe they'll think this sounds really scary but I think they will be a little bit jealous.

   So, be brave, you guys, and get ready for our new adventure!

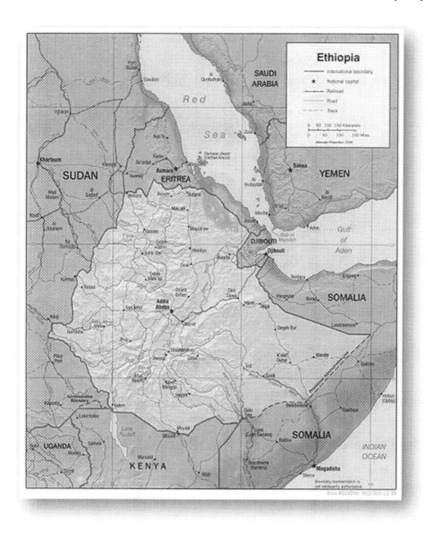

A shaded relief map of <u>Ethiopia</u>, 1999, produced by the U.S. Central Intelligence Agency in public domain. Image source: http://en.wikipedia.org/wiki/File:Ethiopia shaded relief map 1999, CIA.jpg

We were so wrapped up in the excitement of the time that we failed to give credit or enough consideration to my remarkable parents. Wordly and well traveled as they were, they must have been terribly apprehensive but did not let it show. I am sure they were fighting back tears as they saw us off on an icy winter night in New York. We needed three taxis to Kennedy airport to contain all of us and our 17 pieces of unmatched luggage. The taxi I was in skidded and slammed into a center barrier. I got a pretty nasty gash on one leg which we wrapped up for the plane ride. That plane ride was unusual in one respect: we each had 3 seats across so that some sleep was possible. Once in Paris we visited the American Embassy so that the nurse could change my dressing.

Oh, Paris. Truly one of my great loves. We ate dinner on Christmas Eve in a tiny bistro near our hotel. Of course the waiters brought us a "bûche de Noël," I don't remember details of the short stay in Rome, but we had to show the kids the usual wonders: coliseum, in St. Peter's those giants on the ceiling, It was cold but we stayed in a cozy *pensione*. In Athens we traipsed through the old city (the *Plaka*) and met the problem of the little blond boy being grabbed in the street by old ladies.

Then it was time for the flights to our new home.

Chapter One

Ethiopia of all Places

I start with a cast of characters.

You met us briefly in the Introduction. The cast of characters for this series of episodes begins clearly with **Gordon**. He was tall, handsome, slim, yet known to friends and adult family as "Gordo." As mentioned in the introduction, Gordon was adventurous and restless. He was an intellectual, a budding historian, immersed in world events. He possessed a sense of humor which endeared him to everyone and which he never lost, though he was known to get angry at misbehaving children.

Dickie was a well adjusted 11 when the adventure began. He coped fairly well with being dragged from his 6th grade friends back in Illinois. He soon wrote his grandmother "The only culture shock I have received was from plugging my 110 radio into a 220 socket."

Andy was born to march to his own and a different cadence. He was 9. His school and family history included a healthy amount of the devil. During the trip to get to Addis Ababa he managed to elude the family and get lost in Athens. Horrified, we found him unperturbed in the hotel upon return. Discussion of culture shock with plenty of justification as we go along.

Bill was a cherubic 6 year old, cheerful, sociable, athletic. A little young to be taking this all in, we thought. But Billy was never too young for anything. He became apoplectic, however, at being grabbed and kissed by waitresses in Paris, (Daddy and Andy said they'd have loved it) and old ladies in the street in Athens.

To finish the immediate family there was, of course, **me**. I frequently describe my escapades as evidencing more guts than brains. Witness this entire episode.

The Ethiopian staff.

Most beloved was the cook: **Gromu**. A grizzly, skinny, illiterate, sweet character. More about his skills when I talk about food. One of his chief charms was that he called me "memsahib."

Gromu had a son, **Tesfaye,** a year or so older than Dickie, who was always at the house. He and the kids became fast friends. I am not sure how well he spoke English but he appeared to understand most everything, and he certainly taught the boys a great deal of Amharic. Mostly the naughty stuff. He also helped them to improve their soccer.

Mengistu was the No. 2 man. His job was to clean the house, wash the clothes, serve meals, help Gromu, and to keep his eye on the boys when I was out of the house. His English was adequate.

Ademma was the outside man, whose primary task was to take care of grounds and the horses. Much more about that later.

The **zabanya** was the night watchman who arrived at dusk swathed in a dirty white cloak. His job of course was to keep away all of the intruders. He had a "V" shaped reclining wooden chair in which he sat, never supposed to sleep. I don't think I ever knew his name.

Tehruneh was Gordon's driver. He came to get him every morning, and often drove us in the evening to social events. The driver was very instructive about sights, sounds, and culture. Within a day or so after our arrival the family drove into the heart of town with Tehruneh showing us the ropes. I can never forget my three young boys holding up with courage as lepers shoved their stumps and arms into our car windows to gain attention and alms. I was terribly proud of my crew. I honestly didn't think I was scarring them for life. Rather, it was the seed of world understanding.

Later on when I was in the market area, the car was besieged by a woman holding an infant, banging on my window, begging of course. My driver assured me that the woman "rent the baby" to make her begging more effective.

Ethiopia itself.

I started doing research as soon as the assignment was made. Would that there had been a Google in those days. I was fortunate to have been on a European music tour while in college. We had travelled often to Mexico which we found 'muy sympatico.'

But Africa? This was a BIG DEAL!

Ethiopia is Africa's oldest independent country and its second largest in terms of population. Apart from a five-year occupation by Mussolini's Italy, it has never been colonised. It has a unique cultural heritage, being the home of the Ethiopian Orthodox Church - one of the oldest Christian churches - and a monarchy that ended only in the coup of 1974.

Geographically in east central Africa, Ethiopia is bordered on the west by the Sudan, the east by Somalia and Djibouti, the south by Kenya and the northeast by Eritrea.

Most of it is taken up by a central plateau, with many mountains. Addis Ababa (the capital), ranges in altitude from about 7000 ft. above sea level to 9500 ft. Walking up the many hills in town made that fact eminently clear, and playing tennis was an endurance exercise. The Danakil desert contains one of the lowest points on the earth's surface. The Great Rift Valley runs through central Ethiopia, thought to be the site of mankind's origins. Lucy is the name of the nearly complete skeleton of an <u>*Australopithecus*</u> *afarensis.* She was the first nearly complete skeleton recovered for the species, found in 1974. Lucy is about 3.18 million years old, and is called *Denkenesh* in Amharic, the language of the local people.

The country has about 5000 years of history; the earliest possible mention was by the ancient Egyptians. There were obviously many dynasties from the 10th century BC. Tradition holds that all monarchs must trace their lineage back to a king who was the offspring of a seductive relationship between King Solomon and Makeda, the Queen of Sheba. Conversion to Christianity occurred in the 14ᵗʰ century. Ethiopian legends say that when the Queen of Sheba made her famous journey to Jerusalem she was impregnated by King Solomon and bore him a son - a royal prince The name of the prince was Menelik, which means "the son of the wise man". Although he was conceived in Jerusalem he was born in Ethiopia where the Queen of Sheba had returned after discovering that she was carrying Solomon's child. When he had reached the age of twenty, Menelik himself traveled from Ethiopia to Israel and arrived at his father's court. There he was instantly recognized and accorded great honor. After a year had passed, however, the elders of the land became jealous of him. They complained that Solomon showed him too much favor and they insisted that he must go back to Ethiopia. One of his acolytes was said to have stolen the Ark of the Covenant from its place in the Holy of Holies in the Temple. The group of young men did not reveal the theft to Prince Menelik until they were far away from Jerusalem. When at last they told him what they had done he asserted that they could not have succeeded in so bold a venture unless God had willed its outcome. Therefore he agreed that the Ark should remain with them. Thus Menelik brought the Ark to Ethiopia, to the sacred city of Axum, where it has remained ever since.

Modern Ethiopia emerged under Emperor Menelik !!, who established its independence by routing an Italian invasion in 1896. He expanded Ethiopia by conquest. Disorders that followed Menelik's death brought his daughter to the throne in 1917, with his cousin, Tafari Makonnen, as regent and heir apparent. When the empress Taitu died in 1930, Tafari was crowned Emperor Haile Selassie.

All told, at the Battle of Adowa, Ethiopians exposed the mass of lies, untruths and "negrophobic" hatred and racial inferiorization of Africans at the heart of 19th century imperialism. This victory was unprecedented in the archives of modern imperialism and the famous scramble for Africa. The Spectator of March 7, 1896 set the tone and observed mournfully: "The Italians have suffered a great disaster – greater than has ever occurred in modern times to white men in Africa. Adowa was the bloodiest of all colonial battles". Also, the racial dimension of the struggle was unmistakable to the European world.

One thing is incontrovertible about the "second coming" of the Italians, this time in fascist guise. In the 1880s Crispi spoke of a "place in the sun," and plenty of free agricultural land for his army, Fascist propagandists in 1935 spoke of all that and "happy black faces" that await Italian victory.

Haile Selassie secured Ethiopia's admission to the League of Nations in 1923 by promising to eradicate slavery. There were an estimated 2 million slaves in the country in the early 1930s.

There were Muslim incursions as well. About 62% of the population adhere to Christianity, which is Ethiopia's main religion. About 30-35% of the population are Muslim, with other religions covering another 4-5%.

Selassie was an imposing figure despite his small physical size. He surrounded his palace outside and his throne within with living lions. (Sure they were chained, but ominous even so.) They were always stationed on the palace wall. By custom when the Emperor's automobile passed through the streets we diplomats got out of our cars and bowed.

The house assigned to us was not available for a week or so until Gordon's predecessor left. We were quartered in a hotel suite of rooms. I visited the hotel kitchen daily to supervise the construction of the boys' school lunches. No Ethiopian chef had until that time learned to make peanut butter sandwiches. I was enormously relieved when the bivouac was over and we could move into "our" house.

Streets didn't always have names in this strange place where we lived for a brief few months when we first arrived with our three boys in Addis. The street now named (looking at a Google map) Democratic Republic of the Congo street, was known to us as Question Mark Hill. Indeed, it appears on the map to have roughly that shape.

It bore no resemblance to any street we had left behind. Many shacks teeming with family members and animals. There were few "western" dwellings such as ours, a house we (actually the Embassy) rented from an Ethiopian businessman. Two story houses of about six rooms, square boxes undistinguished architecturally. Bathrooms were indoors but functioned poorly. All the houses were surrounded by concrete block walls with broken glass embedded along the top to deter intruders. Between the houses was empty land, not cultivated, used mostly as pathways. There were no sidewalks; the wide street was paved only in two narrow center lanes. Foot traffic, including cattle, donkeys, goats, and sheep plodded along the dusty verge.

There weren't any stores, cleaning establishments, or the usual commercial enterprises. For the most part, the street was lined from top to bottom with tiny "*chica bets*" - chica in Amharic means mud, bet means house. These mud houses were mostly one room tobacco shops. Many had single ladies standing out front. All, without fail, featured a large picture of Haile Selassie (Conquering Lion of the tribe of Judah, elect of God, Emperor of Ethiopia) hanging over the visible shelves or the bed inside.

Selassie on Time Magazine cover, 1930, in public domain.
IMAGE SOURCE: http://en.wikipedia.org/wiki/File:Selassie on
Time Magazine cover 1930.jpg

Being in Addis in those days was like going back in
time. There were a few fairly modern buildings (especially
Afica Hall, which was the seat of the African Union)
and a couple of basic hotels. The streets were roughly
paved except for the thoroughfares. Filing through in
the streets in all parts of the "city" were people, cattle,
donkeys, goats, and sheep. When you neared the palace
wall it was always a good idea to look up top; one or more
lions were sitting up there surveying the situation.

There are centuries old religious traditions and festivals. The national dress was distinctive for both men and women: once white shawls for the men atop knee length shirts over skinny white pants, white *"shamma"* for the women with highly decorative borders. The formal *shamma* looked little like the bedraggled versions of most of the local women. Most people carried umbrellas in the streets against the high altitude sun. The umbrellas had another function in the rainy season, when the downpours rarely ceased.

From the outset we were determined to find and move the family to a more comfortable house. Gordon never could accept the act of the kids moving their bowels while he was in the bathtub or shower. We were five, where the previous tenant had been a bachelor.

We prevailed upon the administrators of our life to secure a house we'd heard about on Queen Elizabeth Street on the way to the British Embassy. By this time we were making moves to change the boys from the American school to a British run International School within walking distance from that house.

The office agreed. Known as the Princess Yetashework Yilma Villa, the house was two stories, with an outside stairway to the second floor. We persuaded them to enclose the stairs. The boys had the downstairs two bedrooms with a bathroom, we had the aerie upstairs with a fireplace and bath. It was weird, but it was perfect. No such thing as a closet. A much larger yard, with the usual fence and gates. A line of servants' buildings along the back wall including a room to dry clothes in the rainy season. There was a "garage" on the side of the house which we later managed to turn into a home for horses. (Our one car didn't need its own house). The yard was scrubby grass, the driveway pebbles and dirt, an acceptable soccer surface. There was a spectacular event one morning in Andy's and Billy's bedroom; it began with a penetrating yell clearly audible in our room. We ran down to find the two young ones standing on their beds, the floor a totally black, writhing carpet of fire ants. Ademma started heaving branches of eucalyptus through their windows onto the floor, telling the boys to stay where they were. In very short order the ants started a swift procession out to whence they came. Eucalyptus leaves are covered with oil glands which the ants clearly dislike. A big lesson about bringing food into the bedroom.

The above-mentioned Princess was a part of the large Selassie clan. We never actually met her. Andy had an occasion to add stripes to his record one day visiting a friend's house. The account is better in his words:

"The other day we were playing at a friend's house. The boy's father (the family is Dutch) is the Director of Shell in Ethiopia. We went in to watch the telly (Saturday it starts at 5:00 pm for children.) Bill and I hesitated to go in because we were kind of dirty. They were having a guest. After I was qualified I went in and met the guest and sat down. Bill was not qualified. When I had to leave my friend's mother told me this was the Crown Prince. For the rest of the day I was thinking 'I've got Princess Ruth down, and the Crown Prince, now all I have to meet is the King'".

I contemplated indulging in some gardening along the long wall on the side. To this end, I wrote my grandmother back in civilization to ask Ernest, her wonderful German gardener, to send me a box of his famous dahlia tubers. He did so. I couldn't believe my luck, and envisioned glory such as I had left behind. I cooked some soil in Gromu's oven to prevent infestations and planted the two dozen tubers. They shortly began to poke green shoots; I was ecstatic. But the inevitable catastrophe loomed. As soon as the shoots gained enough growth to begin to flower, in the course of one day, everything was gone. The cooking hadn't worked. Nematodes.

Just as well. I had not the foresight to realize everything decorative I had or would ever plant in the yard would soon become horse food.

For the most part the climate in the highlands was gorgeous. Temperate, never excessively hot, almost always cool at night. Rainy season something else again. Very cold and grey. I wondered how the multitudes in the rudimentary houses and *chica bets*, with dirt floors, and in the streets ever got dry. Outdoor activities were severely impacted by the incessant pouring, night and day. Deep mud was everywhere. This was pretty significant if you had a household full of roughhousing boys. Another disadvantage : persistent, everywhere, black flies. Never on a picnic could you leave food attractively placed on a tablecloth on the ground. Worse, the flies on the local children, covering their faces, noses and mouths. They seemed to have become accustomed to the scourge.

I found the primitive, unique style of painting immediately appealing. We bought a large woodcarving of the scene showing the Queen of Sheba and Solomon which is in a family house today. A well known painting of the Battle of Adowa hangs in the Alexander Girard Folk Art Museum in Santa Fe showing the two sides riding at each other. I call it the Good Guys vs. the Bad Guys. One group, the Italians, appear only in profile (white faces). The opponents and eventual winners are shown in full face. (The significance is not verified by scholars.)

An image of <u>Tropenmuseum</u> under a <u>Creative Commons license.</u>
IMAGE SOURCE: http://commons.wikimedia.org/wiki/
File:COLLECTIE TROPENMUSEUM De slag bij Adua
TMnr 5956-2.jpg

Gromu did the lion's share of food shopping for our
meals. As a result of our connection with the Embassy,
we had access also to a U.S. Commissary. Essentials such
as peanut butter therefore were available. No meats
or produce. I recall there were also local grocery and
dry goods stores, mostly with empty shelves. The saving
grace was the mercado (obviously, market.)

It was one of the seven wonders of the world.
Separate "aisles" or areas for pots and pans, clay pots,
screws, nuts and bolts, spices, produce, meats hanging on
cleavers, clothing, shoes, you name it. Outdoor markets

have been fixtures all over the world for centuries, but not in the Chicago suburbs (though we had been enamored of them in Mexico.) We began going regularly. I always took visitors, some who were abashed at first. Prominent among the early visitors was an American journalist, Victor Reisel, known for his work in the field of labor, and for having been blinded by an acid attack. He insisted on "seeing" everything.

Bargaining became a fine art. Gordon invented "first gear mentality," and it worked like a charm. The vendor would follow us to our car shouting out his (outlandish) price, which got to a reasonable range as our car went into first gear.

Shortly after arriving in Addis I came home from the mercado with a *gureza* rug – a black and white monkey. The kids loved it. So I followed on with a zebra skin and a heavy wool rug, and had by then bought all the fleas in Addis. When we bought woolen ones, (particularly one with a lion image) one of the main problems was an intense and horrible odor from the rough sheep's wool. We tried many remedies, which eventually worked but required the rugs to remain outside during their treatments. These were small, rough hewn tribal products some of which we continued to use mainly outside, even in the eventual horse barn.

Our experience with pets, which we had promised the kids would feature in our lives, met with varied results. You will soon learn about the "goat." After that was over we bought a few monkeys, invariably deceased within days. (In one letter home I told my mother "monkey #2 deceased. Do not send flowers.") We tried a dog, and then another, with no success. Ethiopian dogs are virtually vermin, never pets, never trained. No experience with a leash or a walk. They sit and howl. So we gave that up. There was a rather bizarre event, a major item in our saga. Andy and Billy never took their eyes off of the various things swooping around up above. Andy had a soul-mate friend who moved, wonder of wonders, to within walking distance of the local slaughter house. To make a long story tolerably short, after a two day sojourn in ecstasy, out visiting this friend, Andy returned to his prosaic dwelling with a new pet, this time a vulture, the loveliest of creatures, alive but injured, on a string. Dickie and Gordon and I had trouble adjusting to the idea, but not so much as the zabanya, who obviously didn't relish the idea of the company out there during the midnight hours. And I really felt like an ass the day I had to admit to the butcher why I wanted particularly slimy meat scraps, in addition to the ground up stuff for our new "puppy." Fortunately the thing recovered from its broken wing and flew away. Andy and Billy were miserably hunched in the yard, eyes on the skies, convinced that each vulture which loomed into sight was "their" vulture who would imminently come back home.

Equally bizarre, during the vulture moments, was an event which befell a colleague of Gordon's. Tragically but also not uniquely, he and his family driving back to Addis from a Sunday excursion, hit and killed a man in the street. By custom, people routinely run right in front of oncoming vehicles, hoping to extinguish the evil spirit. This time the process extinguished him. Following rules of our Embassy, Larry left the scene of the accident but it was clear that the Embassy would have to take care of the burial. To this end, a coffin was obtained in the mercado and stored on our front porch, fittingly next to the vulture.

As far as pets were concerned, we soon hit pay dirt with the horses, but before I get there I want to talk about the food.

Nowadays Ethiopian restaurants proffer their wares in many cities throughout the world complete with authentic presentation, scents, and textures. When my family arrived in Addis Ababa in 1964 there was no familiarity whatsoever with this style of cuisine. (Several members of the family refused to accord it the title of cuisine at all.)

But within the next few weeks we were taken to an Ethiopian restaurant to see what it was all about. Seated around a tall basket, a *mesob,* we awaited plates but plates never came.

Instead, the server brought a large, floppy, pungent spongy bread made from *tef*, a gluten-free grain found only in the Horn of Africa, which she laid all across the mesob. This is called *injera* and is not only plate but eating utensil. Next comes a bowl of *wot,* a stew featuring vegetables, meat, or chicken, lamb or fish, always with whole hard boiled eggs, lentils or other grains The wot is ladled onto the injera. One then tears off a piece of the injera (with the right hand only) and uses it to scoop up a mouthful of wot. The server continuously adds to the conglomeration with more of the same or different types of wot. The seasoning was intense, hot, spicy, and not familiar, but very tasty.

So it goes until one is satiated. But not if you are being hosted by an Ethiopian. The host or hostess keeps feeding morsels of injera/wat – a custom called "*gursha,* or gift" almost down into your throat. an act of friendship and love.

Dickie and Billy soon reached the point of no return with the gursha, and politely protested. Andy, however, held up the honor of the family far longer. On the way to the car after we made our thanks and took our leave, Andy said, "Daddy, put your hand in my pocket." His jacket pocket was full of wet stew; he had maneuvered the mouth-to-pocket action surreptitiously so as not to embarrass his parents or his host. So much for the Brooks Brothers coat but he surely earned his stripes as a diplomat.

The Ethiopian spice is called *berbere* and consists of at least 12 different spices often colorfully layered into jars. To be specific: fenugreek, chiles, paprika, salt, ginger, onion powder, ground cardamom, ground coriander, ground nutmeg, garlic powder, ground cloves, ground cinnamon, and ground allspice. The scent – okay, odor, of this combination is everywhere. It exudes out of pores.

One of the more obvious places it saturates is the paper money carried in pockets. Elevators are unbelievably redolent.

Another dish is raw beef, sometimes marinated. We were astounded at a palace dinner a few months later to see waiters pushing butchers' racks with hanging sides of recently slaughtered animals; many of the guests (undoubtedly no *ferengi*, or foreigners) hacking off pieces with sharp knives.

Tej is a potent honey wine, similar to mead, frequently served in bars, in particular in a *tej bet*. It has a deceptively sweet taste that masks its high alcohol content. *Tella* is a home brewed beer.

Ethiopia holds a credible claim to being the birthplace of coffee and highland-grown coffee is its biggest export. An entire ceremony has grown up around coffee, with beans being roasted and ground in front of the guest.

Travel within the country offered different foods, particularly Assab, on the seacoast in what is now Eritrea, after dropping down the escarpment into the Danakil desert. Halfway down one encounters the Bati camel market, a seldom seen meeting of tribes and goods. Camels are brought from below, merchants descend from the highlands; the bellowing one encounters at the market is indescribable. Maybe like heavy metal concerts of today, to tell the truth.

We never tried to eat camel. But we did find a delicacy down at the Red Sea coast at Assab. Fishermen plied us with tiny crayfish you boil or grill for a very few minutes and eat with delight, shell and all. No more delicious food exists in Ethiopia.

The time had come to learn a new language. I had fortunately had a good grounding in a language other than English; my parents engaged a young Swiss nanny to help my very young mother take care of newborn twins. So we grew up babbling in a combination of French and English and unknowable twin language. My ear became and remained pretty flexible. I studied Spanish in preparation for trips to Mexico when Gordon and I were first married essentially because I could not bear not knowing what people were saying around me. It came pretty easily. I also studied Italian when we were in Ethiopia; because of the Italian influence there were quite a few people around willing to teach the language. (Signor Russo insisted, "Mrs. Winkler, you are speaking French again." But he was very patient.)

But Amharic!! That is another matter indeed. I tried in Washington before our departure to get some language assistance, but found there weren't any of the usual guides or books available from the Foreign Service Institute that they provided to students of important languages such as Chinese, Arabic, Portuguese, etc. And certainly nothing in the marketplace for non-existent tourists to learn to communicate. So I was on my own.

It took quite some time before I began to hear distinctive sounds and differentiate words. I made a pest of myself constantly asking people how to say words and expressions in Amharic.

It is the second-most spoken Semitic language in the world, after Arabic, and the official working language of the Federal Democratic Republic of Ethiopia. Thus, it has official status and is used nationwide. (In recent years other regional languages such as *Wollo* or *Gallinya* have become more prominent, not during the years we were in Ethiopia.) It has been the working language of government, the military, and the Ethiopian Orthodox Church throughout medieval and modern times. Outside Ethiopia, Amharic is the language of some 2.7 million emigrants. (Since the large Ethiopian diaspora to Israel beginning in about 1977 there is a large contingent of Amharic speakers there.) It is written using the Amharic alphabet consisting of some 276 characters, representing consonant sounds headed by a vowel. The script looks to the uneducated eye something like Hebrew.

I plugged away, and was helped in large measure by meeting a young, educated Ethiopian social worker named Alasabu Gebre Selassie. We became close friends. As she helped me struggle with Amharic I started visiting her

Center, which was very near our house. Her clients at the Center were mostly mothers of young children, learning home economics and health management. Somehow I managed to communicate. We started a sewing class, the proximate object was for each mother to make a shirt for one or more of her youngsters. I gave each one a string, to measure around the child's chest. I provided some colorful cloth obtained at the mercado. We added two inches to the knot in the string, cut the cloth from a plain shirt pattern, took turns sewing on the foot powered machines at the Center, and lo and behold, had a fashion show.

On one occasion an American trade show director asked if some of the American women would help in the preparation of an exhibit for the show. He needed some young Ethiopian students to demonstrate and explain common American appliances (á la Betty Furness.) Most of the secondary school students we identified were doing fairly well in English but needed quite a bit of training to use it colloquially to talk about kitchens, refrigerators, etc. During that training I recall learning a few Amharic expressions which didn't adequately translate into the kind of English we needed.

My Mother and Dad came out to visit a short time after our arrival in Addis. They noticed a large group of robed and turbaned clerics on their plane. Upon landing they could not debark until a long red carpet was rolled onto the tarmac up to the stairs of the plane and the

Emperor made his way to the end of it. My dad remarked, "Gordon sure knows how to welcome his guests." There was a convention of Coptic clerics from many parts of the world taking place at the same time as their visit. (They got off first.)

There was a phone call while my parents were visiting and Gordon was briefly in Zambia at a conference. A very familiar voice said, "Mrs Winkler, this is Lowell Thomas. I have just arrived in town from a safari and I wanted to check if there is any news about the health of Ed Murrow." I thought for sure this call was a hoax except that the voice was unmistakable. I quickly called the Ambassador's deputy to apprise him of the eminent visitor and was gratified to take my parents to an elegant dinner to meet the famed journalist. His great friend Edward R. Murrow, Director of USIA, was in failing health and indeed his death occurred soon after this event.

The culmination of the Amharic experience happened after 2 ½ years of living in Addis, when Gordon and I were given a going-away party by a large group of friends at the *tukul,* the famous Addis Ababa restaurant where we had first encountered Ethiopian food. A tukul is a large, straw topped building, round in shape. Gordon gave his thank-yous after being saluted by many friends, told the famous Andy-pocket story and then said to the crowd that Peggy was going to make a talk in Amharic. Alasabu and I had worked for weeks on that speech! I wish I had tape-recorded it, but didn't. I recall it was a success.

The subject of school was very prominent in our Ethiopia experience. We had ripped the three boys out of a very good suburban school back in Illinois, and started them in equivalent grades in the American School in Addis. But we realized we had an option (no, a *duty*) to expose them to a wider variety of colleagues and curriculum choices in the International School where there were students of about 35 different nationalities. And I mentioned earlier that the "English" school was within walking distance of our house of choice on Queen Elizabeth street.

This experience fit the requirement we had of providing a very different scenario for the boys. I asked for contributions so as to show their side of the story. Andrew's refreshed my memory as to exactly where we lived and what was the boys' route to school. In those days we were lucky to be able to let them trudge the neighborhood through unpaved streets and alleys on their own and deal with the local kids who occasionally yelled at the "*ferengi*."

Here is what I got from Number One Son, by decree now Richard:

"When I was 12 years old Queen Elizabeth visited my school. First thing every morning the entire school had Assembly: hundreds of students of all ages and ethnicities packed standing in a big musty room to hear announcements, news, schedule changes, etc. At least once a week some kid would faint or barf, the latter signaled by the sound of the rapid effort of others around the sick kid scrambling to get out of range.

The headmaster making most of the pronouncements was a priggish, authoritarian, scary guy named Leslie Casbon. Straight out of Evelyn Waugh. Students who got in trouble got "caned" by him in his office. My younger brother was one of the few white kids to get caned. Later we heard that the older brother of an Arab kid who had been caned came back to the school and beat up Casbon at Assembly. Unfortunately we had already left by then.

This was during the Cold War and there was a Czech kid who sat in front of me who was my nemesis. He used to mess with my geometry kit and say things like "you Americans all you do is watch TV and eat smashed potatoes." One day I'd had enough and when he reached back to harass me I stabbed him in the hand with my sharpened pencil; the lead snapped off and stuck up out of his knuckle about $\frac{1}{2}$ inch. He didn't bother me again.

I was an indifferent student easily distracted by the cute British girls in my classroom. All the teachers were English; one of mine was a woman who was probably anti-American because she usually said something snide

or sarcastic when she handed back my papers. At the
end of every year the entire school was given a "trivial
knowledge" test. One year I won and was summoned up
to the front of the assembly to get my award: a Penguin
paperback book called "3 Corvettes." My teacher was
the one who gave out that award so even though I was
shocked to hear her call my name out I somehow managed
to stay cool and act blasé as if this was no big deal.

Anyway, while we lived there the Queen made a
state visit to Ethiopia during which she came to visit the
school. There was some pre-war British army connection
to the founders of the school so we were on the official
itinerary. This was a big deal as you can imagine. All
of the students got dressed up and were arranged by
country around the sports field sort o like the opening
of the Olympics. There were about 30 or so countries
represented so it was kind of impressive. And hot. We
waited out there for her scheduled noon arrival sweating
in our coats and ties. And waited. She was at least three
hours late when it clouded over and began to rain. And
rain. We were rushed off the field into the assembly
hall. I was towards the back and could see steam literally
rising from the mass of overdressed, sweaty kids.
The Queen and Prince Phillip finally arrived but all I
remember about the rest of the day was feeling itchy
from my wool pants (I still can't wear wool pants), woozy
and hoping I would not throw up."

So much for the intellectual advantages of this international education.

There is a possibly apocryphal addition to this story. Andy says that on the day of the visit, the Prince stooped down to shake his American hand and asked "What do you want to be when you grow up?" Andy says he looked way up to the top of the Prince and said, "tall".

Out of curiosity and a way of avoiding the usual American wife chore of attending to the day to day wishes of the Ambassador's wife (disparagingly described as attending teas and making cookies) I researched admission to the Haile Selassie University. To no one's surprise I was accepted as a credit student. I spent two years there, most of which was of substantial value. One of my professors was an Israeli whose class was entitled "Islamic Institutions." He became a very close friend of our family and the information therein a strong foundation for our later postings and the rest of my life. "British Imperialistic History" was another of my favorite courses. Intensive study of the Boer War, which was a subject about which I doubt I'd have read on my own. And of particular great value because since, many of our best friends have been. by good fortune. and are South Africans.)

One of my professors was a disgrace, specifically an Ethiopian gentleman who will remain nameless, whose course was entitled "Geo-Political History of Africa" and who rarely showed up to lead class. The best thing about that class was a rabid Ugandan student who questioned me resentfully and continually about why my country worked. It was fun dealing with that situation. My litany was centered on our single language, despite the not-so-subtle variations such as Southern, Chicago and Brooklyn accents. The linguistic map of Africa helped me make my point; it was an insert in one of my African history books. The jigsaw puzzle of little pieces of language showed why national unity was (and remains) an impossibility anywhere on the African continent. Evading the influence of tribalism proved to be a phantom desire, and has continued to be throughout the world.

My experience as a student helped me make a contribution as a listening post at the University. I will have to admit I passed on many of the rumblings of my co-students to Gordon's office, but compared to our later experience there was no significant undercurrent of dissatisfaction among the student body with the government or the Emperor. It proved to be too soon in the new spirit of *Uhuru* for any rebelliousness to emerge.

An illustration of my daily life when I wasn't going to school gleaned from a letter I wrote to my sister:

"Schedule: (abbreviated)

8:30-10:30 Drove a photographer to shoot 5 scenes of American women engrossed in some welfare activity.

12:00   French class

4:00   Pony club. Last week I tried to teach all
of my babes how to hold the reins via do-
it-yourself method, I made each of them
practice on a piece of plastic clothes line
looped around a fence post. When they
learned I let them ride. Only one kid fell off.

6:00   shower

8:00   30 people for dinner. This one got a little
out of hand. Made the dessert yesterday
afternoon, flowers just needed to be
spruced up from Wednesday's dinner. Gromu
has the rest of the worry. (Fillets, cooked
outside, 2 kinds of wot without meat because
it's a fast day and 75% of the guests are
Ethiopian probably none of whom fast.) The
dishes won't match, but the Nigerian is
bringing hi-life records, *gid-yellim (what the
hell ___)*."

     Sundays Gordon's driver was not on duty, so soon
after our arrival Gordon drove the car (warily) to the
excursion of the day. One of the very early ones was to
get a pet. Ordinary people may settle for a dog (more
later) but we had decided to get a goat. In Amharic,
"*fiyal*" means goat. One reason for the choice was to get
the grass cut around the house. This was in the days of

house #1 on Question Mark Hill. Behind the house was a steep hill leading to huts above: families, snarling dogs, chaos. No fences, of course.

We got a general idea of where to go from Gromu, not yet knowing the lay of the land. And of course we had no clue as to how to enact a transaction in Amharic.

So we found a passel of animals out there a ways, and selected a fiyal. I recall they bound the legs and put him or her in the back of the car. It looked a bit odd, with a fat tail. It was decidedly a dirty animal, which we agreed to clean up with blasts from a hose.

It seemed to like our house when we let it out. It let us clean it up a little, and began to chomp on the unruly vegetation. We decided it was a girl, and named her "Elemy" after a good friend of Billy's (whose name was Emily) back home.

When the night watchman (the 'zabanya') came we learned a couple of Amharic words. It seems we had not bought a fiyal, we had bought a "*beg*," a sheep. (No farming in either of our backgrounds.) It bore no relation to picture book notions of a lamb. The zabanya looked at us in disbelief. It was then we learned the word "*dankworo*," which means stupid. (Us.)

Before too long we heard a terrible racket out back at the bottom of the hill. It seems the dog population from above was coming down to take bites out of Elemy. Her flanks and back were bloodied and matted. Of course we were horrified but what to do? We certainly couldn't call the authorities or take a complaint up the hill to the unknown neighbors.

Last straw in this folly. We gave the sheep to the zabanya to take home for an upcoming holiday featuring a sacrifice.

One of the closest places to visit on Sundays was called the hippo pool. It was at a town called Ambo, not far from Addis. We looked forward to Sundays and went often. Ambo featured a river, a large pool fed by a hot spring, so hot the water was pumped up to 100 feet or so and dropped down into the pool to cool it enough for swimming. We always took a picnic and made a day of it. Many of our friends went regularly so the days were always enjoyable.

From the banks of the river we watched with fascination a collection of hippos giving each other glancing blows and diving up and under the water. There was also a large clan of crocodiles. For these obvious reasons, nobody ventured into the river. One day one of the crocs with a mighty jump landed in the swimming pool. The pool emptied immediately of all Winkler boys and other swimmers.

Photo: Victoria Whelan

One event relative to this discussion occurred shortly after we got to Addis. Gordon's office received word from the director of the Peace Corps that a volunteer had been killed by a crocodile in a river down-country. Of course all volunteers had been warned by their administrators and by the local residents not to swim in rivers, yet one heedless young man ventured in to go across. The croc was later shot, the remains obtained from its stomach, and sent to his parents in the United States. That certainly underlined the danger!

We made it a point to travel often around the country. USIS, or the United States Information Service, as my husband's office was called, distributed information about America and films to a lot of out-of-the-way rural places. One night we were in a village where Gordon's staff assistant set up a large screen to show a movie. *On the screen* an actor left a room and closed a door behind. A large number of people in the outdoor audience ran behind the screen to see where the person had gone. I am not fabricating that story!

The second group of the Peace Corps volunteers arrived in Addis about when we did. Peace Corps II was a wonderful group of young people. We had occasion to get to know the ones living in Addis and often stayed with the ones in towns we visited around the country. We carried sleeping bags and slept on their floors. No Motel 6's available, and the Peace Corps was welcoming. Our children became very close friends of children of Peace Corps staff, attending the same school, riding together, etc.

I had heard that Haile Selassie, attending JFK's funeral, had been asked if he wanted help in erecting a memorial to the slain President. He responded "We need no memorial beyond the 342 of Kennedy's children who are now serving in our country."

After the aforementioned official visit of Queen Elizabeth II to Haile Selassie her entourage took a trip to the mountains for a view of the utterly gorgeous scenery. In all of my travels I have seen nothing to equal the Ethiopian highlands; apparently the Queen's advisers had been so advised. After she had left we had occasion to pass by the site where her staff had staged a overnight stay, complete with whitewashed boulders to delineate the viewing area. And two whitewashed flagsticks, inasmuch as the Emperor accompanied the Queen and Prince Phillip. (An unusual sight in the wilderness.) A sense of the vastness of the gorges and mesas stretching indefinitely was brought home when a young student who had been identified by his teachers as a candidate for an exchange visit to the United States told us when he reached Addis that the trip started with a trek lasting 17 days until he reached the nearest *road.*

A large part of our mission involved educational exchange. Students were sent every year at high school level to study in the states. The roster of national leaders around the world consists of substantial numbers of those exchange students.

An exciting day dawned. I was going to make a stab at acquiring a horse. So I went over to the polo grounds (a dusty, huge, uneven field of stones, hunks of "grass," where I had heard there were often horses for sale. I must have had Ademma with me, in case I found something which needed to be brought home. Wishful thinking!

Lots of horses available. My eye hit on a pretty ugly, yellowish but sturdy and interesting large fellow which I decided to investigate. He had a type of scrofula down one side of his face. Something drew me nevertheless. The owner provided a saddle and I got on; it was love at first feel. I knew this would be perfect for Gordon and whichever of the kids would want to ride. His gaits were gentle as a rocking horse, his mouth was accepting of the bit, the strength and willingness were

obvious. There was a prominent backbone with saddle
sores which did present a problem. I had a hunch a
different saddle could be found, which turned out to be
true; a member of the military found us a McClellan which
sat upon the flanks on pontoons, avoiding pressure on the
backbone. The horse was ours.

I introduced "Mustard" to the family and they
agreed we had a winner. We had fitted out the shed on
the side of the house with eucalyptus poles and boxes
to fashion 3 stalls. Mustard went gently into the first.
He had the run of the grounds when not put "to bed"
and often came to the kitchen door to get carrots from
Gromu. We got one great picture of him with almost half
his body inside the kitchen. Later on I took him with me to
the British Embassy where I taught at the Pony Club. Just
about every young one wanted a chance to ride the big guy.

Andy and Mustard

But we could not do with only one. So I went again, this time for me. I am very particular about *my* horseflesh; it has to be pretty. Preferably black. This time I saw a more refined looking animal, clearly a tribal horse but handsome. He may well have had some Arabian blood. There was, however, a huge problem! The horse had probably been abused on the left side of his head, and spooked big time if anyone approached on the left. That happens to be the side from which one mounts a horse, of course. The owner helped me to mount from the right, I urged the beast to take a few steps and to go around the grounds. Immediate connection; I determined to get around the disadvantage.

So "Chocolate, pronounced Choko-latte." came home as well. Ademma did not report any problem leading him home, as long as he led from the right. Chocolate went into stall number 2. He was terribly nervous and a bit scary. He began to relax when I hung my pants in his stall so he could get used to me and his new place. I could not groom his left side for a long time. When I took him anywhere and someone approached to talk to me I had to warn vociferously not to come at the left side of Chocolate's head. Mustard's proximity must have been reassuring because Chocolate eventually became a bit more placid.

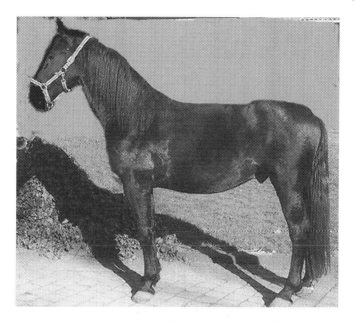

Ethiopian horses were never shod. Their hooves accommodated whatever paths we took, rocks, sand, or gravel. One day we were advised to have Mustard's hooves trimmed, they were indeed too long. Ademma summoned a man who arrived with knives to do the job. He had to knock Mustard out; he would not stand still for his pedicure.

The third horse to finish out the "stable" was a tiny grey pony with perfect conformation we got for the boys. The only problem was that Salty had no intention ever to stop. More strength in that mighty mite than you could believe. Andy and Billy were willing to try, not Dickie. Our "stable" was full.

Horse food consisted of alfalfa which appeared in the street piled on donkeys which Ademma ushered in through the gate.

Gordon and I began riding regularly out in the eucalyptus forests behind our house. It was glorious. Gordo would call from the office and say "saddle Mustard." He saddled his own horse as often as he had diapered his babies. We would return from a two hour ride and finish off at the "polo" field so Mustard could run and run for another while. A great brute indeed. There were some importune meetings out in the forests, specifically one with an "incredible naked man." By and large people were pleasant and friendly.

The importance of eucalyptus in Ethiopia cannot be overestimated. An import from Australia, it was introduced about 1895 by King Menelik II. Menelik encouraged its planting around Addis, the new capital city, because of the massive deforestation that had taken place around the city for firewood and timber. It is a

tree that adapts to a variety of environments. One of
the great advantages of the eucalyptus is that it is fast
growing, requiring little attention and when cut down it
grows up again from the roots; a whole new stand can be
harvested sooner than every ten years. We would ride
out one week in a dense group of eucalyptus trees, the
next week it was all gone. But soon growth began anew.
The immature trees look completely different from the
mature trees. Among the distinctive aspects of eucalyptus
is its pervasive pungent odor. This moved quickly into our
sensory memory. Even now when I come across it from
somewhere, it evokes these long ago recollections.

In addition, there were frequent horse events on
the weekends when horse friends from other embassies
and some of the Ethiopian military took long rides. The
culmination of this kind of activity took place just before
we left Addis after about two and a half years; the
Ambassador from Britain sent out an invitation to a picnic
on a far flung mountainside.

Not your usual picnic!

The grooms (Ademma and counterparts) walked the
horses for hours to arrive at the destination. We drove
out, of course, mounted and rode for another couple
of hours. As we dismounted, drinks were offered by a
bevy of servants, and a sumptuous luncheon was served
under tents at long tables atop Persian rugs. At the end
of lunch the Ambassador ordered the tables cleared

and laid with fresh linen so that he could jump his horse across them at a dead run.

Perhaps the most spectacular trip we took was to the rock-hewn churches of Lalibela. Now quite often visited, at the time it was only beginning to be restored for visitors by an Ethiopian princess.

Bete Giyorgis (Church of St. George), Lalibela, Ethiopia taken by Bernard Gagnon under a Creative Commons license. IMAGE SOURCE: http://en.wikipedia.org/wiki/File:Bete Giyorgis 03.jpg

The predominant religion of Ethiopia is Coptic Christianity, which reappeared after the rise and rapid expansion of Muslim Arabs in the early decades of the 7th century. Around the middle of the 11th century a notable Christian ruler named King Lalibela arose in the Amhara region of the highlands. According to legend, a dense cloud of bees surrounded the Prince at the time of his birth. His mother chose the name Lalibela, meaning "the bees recognize his sovereignty." Lalibela was given orders from God to build a new Jerusalem with churches in a unique style. Assisted by angels he and his brother built twelve extraordinary churches over a period of twenty five years. Each church is sculpted, both inside and out, directly from the living bedrock of the earth. The walls of the trenches and courtyards contain cavities and chambers filled with mummies. The churches are still used for worship today, many are filled with richly painted biblical murals.

When we decided to visit this wonder of the world we managed to find a plane which landed us upon a flat area down below the area of the rock churches. We were met by a jeep, but its driver failed to manoeuver the uphill trip. The engine simply couldn't make it. Ever resourceful, the driver turned the jeep around and went up backwards.

There was a rudimentary hostel where we stayed the night of our visit before heading down on donkeys to meet the returning plane. The donkeys had no trouble

managing the decline going forwards. Mine decided
half way to lie down in the river (which I enjoyed as an
excellent means of keeping cool during a two hour ride in
the blistering African noonday sun.) I was baptized, you
might say.

Gordon on local transportation

We had purchased a large 5 person tent prior
to our venture to Ethiopia, and used it often camping
particularly at Lake Langano which we accessed in our
VW van, climbing up rocky roads to reach the side of
the lake. Of course we would be met and surrounded by
youngsters clamoring to be hired as our camp guard. We
always hired one or two to keep the others away. We
became proficient in planning provisions for the one to
three day trips. Except for one occasion when we were

accompanied by a prominent Ethiopian artist who asked upon arrival, "Where is the scotch?" Oops, we goofed that time. He got into his car and went to the nearest village and brought some back. We had never forgotten that essential before.

Everything left over when we broke camp disappeared into the forest, cans, bottles, etc. They became valuable commodities for the locals. We always knew the locals were near but just out of sight. In the middle of one night the drumming became louder and Gordon was sure they were coming for his prized Sears Roebuck boots, the envy of all of the children.

Andy became obsessed with shooting a hawk after seeing one stuffed and mounted on the school principal's wall. He prevailed upon me to visit a taxidermist to prepare for the eventuality. I told him not to live in a world of dreams, to which he retorted "they aren't dreams, they're plans." On one camping trip with some of our close friends, our camping companion had brought rifles for that purpose. It finally happened, much to my displeasure, and I have to admit that a prouder youngster never existed.

On another trip one of our party, not our family, shot a wild pig. We stopped at a restaurant on the way home to have the proprietor prepare it for our dinner. There was a restaurant/bar at the railroad station in

Addis whose owner frequently served us wild game, including boar. Delicious.

We took advantage of school vacations to travel both in Africa and north to Beirut, Greece, Hungary and Yugoslavia for what was called "rest and rehabilitation."

The principal trip in Africa took place in our first summer, when the rains in Addis never ceased and I thought I would surely go mad. I took the boys to the Kenyan resort town called Malindi for a beach holiday, before Gordon would get away to meet us in Nairobi for a safari (no guns!) to a couple of game parks. Malindi was small, primitive, and very appealing in those days. The waters of the Indian Ocean were sparklingly clear, and beckoned snorkelers. Who would have thought we Chicago folk would be found endlessly bottoms up looking at a wonder world of tropical fish just underneath. We spent hours in that pursuit and compared notes when we came up for air.

We found Nairobi congenial and peaceful. In writing this I must remind readers that this was in 1964. Time has not been kind.

We made our arrangements for a van with a driver named David, to travel down to Amboseli and then to the Ngorogoro crater, traveling west to Lake Victoria. This itinerary got us to Kenya, Tanganyika as it was then, and Uganda. The recollections have remained indelibly in all

of our minds: visiting with the imperial Masai, driving
through herds of elephant, driving down into the gorge
to the bottom of the crater with the "White Hunter"
driver pointing out Old George, the rhino with his five
feet (he let the boys figure out for themselves that the
fifth appendage wasn't a foot). One of the highlights
for me was the vision in Amboseli of a giraffe running.
The animal's brain sends a message to the feet which
eventually gather themselves to commence a loping
gait nobody can ever see in a zoo. Utter freedom from
restraint. Its opposite: one day during a stop on our
trip across Kenya I climbed up the sides of a truck
being driven across the plain. It was careening wildly,
temporarily stopped on our route. Then looked down
upon a rhinoceros captured for some reason, and damned
unhappy about it.

Our lodgings in the parks were far from luxurious
as these safari camps are described today. However, in
the tent camp in Amboseli a porter brought a canvas tub
into the tent and buckets of water for memsahib to have
a hot bath; the boys and Papa had to shower outside in
the trees. Memsahib loved that luxurious touch.

We headed west. We saw a sturdy sign in Arusha
with directional arrows pointing in many directions. It
stated that we were standing on the equator. Arrows
pointed to New York, London, Paris, Alaska, Singapore,
Tokyo, etc. The geography lesson for the day was clear
to all.

Having driven across the Serengeti to Uganda
we had to visit the pygmies. The boys had hysterics as
one of the pygmy ladies, about 4 feet tall, took a shine
to their father and wouldn't leave him alone. The pygmy
lady, without top dressing of course, demonstrated the
result of carrying around breastfeeding babies; one of
her breasts looked to be in the usual place while the
other dangled close to her waistline.

Arriving at Lake Victoria, covered in dust and hot,
we stopped for a brief cleanup. We knew we shouldn't
go swimming in the lake, because of the prevalence
of bilharzia snails in the reeds, which caused the
debilitating disease of shistosomiasis. We tried to find

a spot free of reeds and dashed in to soap up quickly, hoping the snails wouldn't find us or the soap would kill them. I admit I worried about the possible residual danger to the kids, knowing the shistosomes brooded in bodies for years. I breathed easier when the State Department doctor pronounced them free of any signs of the disease at the physicals which took place later upon return to the United States.

We had our share of illness, nothing terribly serious. I had a spate of West Nile Fever, or spinal meningismus. Fortunately the Public Health Service and the Peace Corps doctor administered morphine for the paralyzing headache. The illness probably came from a mosquito which hitched a ride from the port at sea level on a truck up to the highlands. Gordon had a pretty severe attack of asthma during which the entire hospital ceased its perennial blasting on doctor's orders. Both parents also had cases of hepatitis (in my case accompanied by giardia, ugh!!) we probably got from dipping into mountain pools on Sunday hikes in the mountains. Billy later had a tapeworm which was a pretty disgusting event and took several days to resolve.

The second summer in Addis we decided to head out of Africa, north to Greece and Eastern Europe via Beirut.

Beirut was stunning, classy, justifiably known as the Paris of the Middle East. We had one stop to make at

the American Hospital to remove stiches in my forehead.
I had smashed my head into Chocolate's trying to jump
a log in the driveway. That errand didn't take long. In
minutes we were walking on the boardwalk discovering a
local institution: the gyro. Hard to believe these days,
but this was new to westerners in the 1960s. We had
foreign service friends-of-friends to visit in a stunning
apartment above the coast. We were insulated from the
threat of the horrible wars just on the horizon even as
we became aware of the schisms in the society.

After Beirut a brief stop in Athens. The Athens
Festival was on but the Berlin Philharmonic was sold
out. A friend wangled us invitational tickets in the third
row of the Herod Atticus theatre at the foot of the
Acropolis. Five or six seats in the front row remained
vacant except for red velvet cushions. Shortly King
Constantine and his bride arrived, he in black trousers,
shining black shoes and a short sleeved white open shirt.
We agreed he was a lot less formal than "our" king.

Then we headed for the islands. The highlight was
clearly Mykonos, sparkling blue and white, charming curvy
streets. We arrived without a reservation, as do a lot of
tourists. Locals meet every boat offering lodging in their
homes. What could have been better? We kept the boys
active by inventing a game, or rather they did, in which
they start out from the same location and find a stated
destination following different routes. Before long they
had become good tour guides.

A friend in Addis had offered his Paros house
for a short stay, and we went there after some glorious
Mykonos days. The house lacked electricity; we stocked
up on candles and flashlights. The island lacked a single
English speaker, and we needed to shop for the kitchen.
Out came the language books and I crammed Greek into
my head. Those are the kind of experiences I love, more
so than did my husband. I was never embarrassed to
make a fool of myself.

The outstanding experience in Geece was a visit
to a remote monastery. We drove through the plains of
Thessaly to "see a few rocks," as Billy put our anticipated
visit to *Meteora*. He subsequently ate crow because we
had an experience there that topped most any we had
had before. We decided to climb what seemed like an
endless stairway carved in the rock only to come upon
a door, which suddenly, creakingly, and all by itself,
opened. Naturally we went through, and saw attached
to the door a wire leading up somewhere. We continued,
up more stairs, and were met at the summit by a layman
who ushered us into a room hanging out over the cliff.
He bade us to sit down at a table where there were
five glasses of water, 2 glasses of Ouzo, and candy for
the children. Then an aged monk appeared and sat down
with us and began a conversation which lasted about an
hour. The non-monk and I spoke French, I translated
for us and he in Greek to the old monk. This was a one
of a series of 14th century monasteries, built during
a period of religious oppression, and dying out one by

one. The non-monk then took us to see a shack out back lined with shelves containing neatly arranged skulls of all of the deceased monks from the 14th century to the present day.

Each time we stopped in cities in Greece we were spectators at demonstrations in the streets, not realizing this was the wave of the future. I wrote home that we had two signs prepared, so as to be able to participate. One said "Papandreou" on one side and "Tsirimokos" on the other, the other sign was temporarily left blank in case the king came up with somebody equally interesting.

After our stay in Greece we flew to Belgrade, and found it a sad, rude, ugly surprise. We could not change our reservations to leave in fewer than 4 days. But after that disappointment Budapest looked even better than it otherwise would. We stayed in the famous old Gellert hotel, with a spa in the basement.

Everybody in Budapest swims somewhere during their workday, leaving their homes with small gym bags. In the Gellert spa we realized why. It was a cavernous, dark, dank space with numerous pools designated work or play. The boys loved the huge pool with waves that came on with a timer to simulate the ocean. Other pools are strictly for sprint and long distance swimmers. A notable feature of the space comprised a number of tables where large Hungarian men and women pummelled vast quantities of fat on copious bodies.

Every trip to the spa was followed by a trip to one of the notable chocolaterias, especially Vorosmarty, where pink-checked spa-pounded ladies indulged in sinful, gorgeous confections with their small dense coffees.

In 1954 the U.S. government had passed a Food Relief Act which distributed tons of food aid to needy countries after the war. As a result of the Act Americans traveling to Hungary luxuriated in unbelievably low currency exchange rates. One particular benefit accrued to Billy, then aged seven, having his first massage ever in the Gellert spa. "Daddy, I loved it so much! Can I have another one?" Quite an indulgence for a little spoiled American child, back-to-back massages. Not too terrible, inasmuch as each massage cost the U.S. equivalent of six cents.

Meals in Budapest were splendid. A distinct relief after our disappointment with any and all food in Greece.

They also afforded us a chance to talk with waiters, frequently inquiring about how they felt about their politics. A few were very candid about their feelings about the Communists. One night we ended dinner with a wonderful confection called "Touros Palatchinten," a crepe filled with a delicate cheese, sprinkled with powdered sugar. A few evenings later I stayed in the hotel with a small disturbance in the belly, and Gordon took the boys back over to the same restaurant for a replay of that desert. Not facile with the language, they tried to describe with vast arm motions that they wanted something that was rolled. After a while they were presented with huge plates of kebabs. They wouldn't let me off duty after that.

Back to Addis for the wind-down. Amazing how fast two and a half years flew by. A short spate of time for sure, but an indelible effect on us all. We had amassed a large number of friends, Ethiopians and ex-pats, the Ethiopian staff, colleagues, the horses. We had to say goodbye to all. -- the inevitable aspect of our peripatetic lifestyle.

We were not inclined at all to end the adventure so we awaited word of the next posting. Pretty sure it would be in Africa again, but where?

Chapter Two

Across the Continent From the brisk highlands to the sultry west

There was a big change in the offing. We were assigned to Ghana and were faced with the prospect of splitting up the family, There was not an appropriate secondary school in Accra; the British, who had run the country for years, habitually sent their sons and daughters "home" to a proper English school as young as eight or ten years of age.

Colleagues of Gordon's had been assigned to Rome and had entered a son in a branch of a Connecticut. preparatory school. They were enthusiastic about "St. Stephens" so we pursued the application procedure to have Dick admitted in the fall of 1966. (When this kid was little he would have nothing whatsoever to do with a tomato or a dish containing tomatoes. Sending him to Rome made him get over his vexing obsession.) Although far away from "home" and his own parents he would have these friends *in loco parentis*, which was very comforting.

Seth was the same age as Dick and they were good friends.

Dick had to get to school before we traveled to West Africa. With trepidation we put him on a plane by himself. Other good friends were to meet him at the Rome airport and get him to school. We hardly had time to hear about how he settled in before we embarked by ship to stop in Italy and see for ourselves. We assigned homework to Andy and Billy; they were not enthusiastic or cooperative. We found Dickie in an adapted Roman Villa in the Parioli district, quite happy. The students had access to all of Rome and we envied him no end. (On a subsequent trip to visit his family in Accra he was heard to announce that "we" had had enough of Africa.) He sent regular reports of grades and stories about treasure hunts across the city; we were sure we had done the right thing.

Arrival in Accra, housing again proved to be a problem. We were assigned to a house which would clearly not work as "representational," i.e. a place to entertain guests as often as would be required, so I embarked on a search for a substitute. I think I covered the waterfront, and eventually found the right spot. The first night we slept well (at sea level) until the boys yelped, "Hey Rents, look what's on the wall." We didn't have to travel to their rooms, our own had a few green and yellow gecko lizards crawling up and down the walls, nodding their little heads, perfectly charming once you got used to the idea. Their job was to take care of other less welcome creatures.

In the morning we met the "kuku", Philippe, whose main claim to fame was his infatuation with mayonnaise. He really was a terrible cook, but he spoke enough English (this was a British colony, after all) and professed a willingness to learn. I had to hide the mayonnaise.

Due to the presence of insects and their larvae absolutely everything worn on the body needed to be ironed after washing. West African heat and humidity made for many daily changes of clothing. This required a "wash man," (The insects would lay their eggs in clothing hanging up to dry and soon hatch them into nasty larvae which burrowed and produced large and painful boils.) Robert was a handsome and willing addition to our household. He had a lot of character embodied in a hat made of a lion's mane, which he wore religiously on his

day off walking in the streets of town. One day I asked
Robert where Philippe was. His answer: "He go walka-
walka,- he go come." You judge the proficiency of his
language. I knew exactly what he meant. It was a miracle,
after the experience in Ethiopia, to be living without
flies. Nobody seemed to come up with the answer to their
complete absence, everybody rejoiced,

The cost of living was relatively outrageous,
affecting our search for a residence. After moving
twice, however, we found a house, and made an immediate
connection to the owner, a leading obstetrician/
gynecologist in the community. By coincidence, we had
years before had lunch with his brother, a prominent
judge, in Chicago at the Drake Hotel. The house was airy
and large, with an interior courtyard growing a jungle in
huge pots. The library was air conditioned; ceiling fans
worked all day in the other rooms. We had a short wave
radio in the library which sputtered news items. One day
I heard mention of Martin Luther King, using the word
"was." "Oh God no", I screamed, "Not him too." Bobby
Kennedy's horrible tragedy preceded that by a couple
of months. It was hard to be so removed from home
when things like that happened. but we could hardly have
helped our society to be more rational.

Upstairs bedrooms also had big fans. Everything
fine, except the house was not waterproof; after
numerous occasions when we mopped for hours we
became conditioned like Pavlov's dogs. When the sky

turned grey and the wind began to blow we packed the doors with rags and towels. A bit disconcerting in the middle of dinner parties – one evening when the landlord was a dinner guest and the storm threatened he was far more embarrassed than I was. Actually the climate was slightly less humid than we had been led to believe and there was a persistent breeze making temperature relatively comfortable. The grounds were large, and I hired a genius of a gardener who was suspected of having grown *celery* on his previous job. The whole place was planted in grass and "we are green, green, green." We had all of the amenities except for a telephone. That was a real problem, which took almost a year to solve. When it finally arrived and was installed and worked, I sent out a birth announcement, a picture of a stork carrying a telephone named "75443."

Foodstuffs were in short supply with shelves in local markets varying from sparse to empty. One local superstore prominently displayed crystal water glasses at the equivalent of $312 a glass. By contrast, great, glorious avocadoes and pineapples were plentiful. And haircuts were cheap.

Understanding and dealing with the currency was confounding. A little over a year before, the Ghanaian pound was taken out of circulation and replaced with "*cedis* and *pesewas.*" At the rate of cedis 2.40 to the pound, or 8 shillings fourpence to the cedi. The cedi was equivalent to $1.17. The trouble was, nobody sold anything in cedis, they quoted in shillings. Never having absorbed shillings, I was at a loss. After reporting this dilemma to the home folk I reported that returning from the beach we had bought 5 lobsters for 10 shillings, alias a cedi twenty five, or $1.46. Everything is relative.

Apart from the cost of housing, meat, and just about everything else, how was Ghana?

> November 20, 1965 I wrote home: "How's Ghana? Ghana is one great grin. Its citizenry is happy. visibly relieved of the despair known under the Nrumah regime "(Kwame Nkrumah was deposed a year before.) One is struck immediately with the unparalleled kindness and courtesy of the people. After what we've seen elsewhere in Africa, in Europe and at home, the traffic manners stand out strikingly. It is a common occurrence for a car to stop so as to let you in line, or cars to stop immediately to help with directions and repairs. The police are disciplined, efficient and courteous. Everybody is. We think it's going to be a torrid relationship."

Until 1957 Ghana was under British rule. Known then as the Gold Coast, its succession of Ashanti and other tribal chiefs pushed their colonial rulers for independence. Finally came the pronouncement in late

1956 that Ghana would be the first African colony to achieve independence.

"Then came the earthquake of emotion that made the sea hesitate from breaking on the beach. That, some say brought a rain of coconuts tumbling from the trees. That made the very lizards scurry for cover. That, some mothers will tell you, made their unborn babies kick with joy in their wombs..."

Dr. Kwame Nkrumah had been imprisoned (by the British) for seven years. When he took office as Prime Minister there was every expectation that the new land would thrive. Yet his costly demands for pomp and splendor, his banning of any opposition, his usurpation of traditional tribal authority, all combined to erode the promise. He was overthrown in a *coup d'etat*. A great statesman, J. B. Danquah (whose widow became one of my very good friends) wrote that Nkrumah had condemned his nation to many years of political and economic agony. When we arrived shortly after the overthrow we found people joyously relieved.

There were 70 tribal languages spoken in the country (size slightly smaller than Oregon) the principal of which were *Fante, Twi,* and *Ga.* I must admit I never learned a word of any of them. Most, if not all, of the warm friends we made in the next two and a half years had been educated in England (at "Oxbridge") or in a renowned secondary school in Accra called Achimota.

(To my knowledge there were no non-Ghanaian students enrolled in this very demanding institution.) Our Ghanaian friends were by and large well educated and established professionals. One in particular soon became the attorney general, others were judges and doctors (including our landlord).

Many of these friends had conducted further professional education in the United States. The language of education was English and the curricula indomitably British. I had a disturbing experience in a later trip into the rural countryside. Looking over the shoulders of students in middle school, I found them studying the agricultural produce of East Anglia! Now, really.

Andy and Billy enrolled in the Ghana International school, which stunned us with the hours of 7:30 to 12 noon. Andy wrote to Grandpa:

"I really like it very much and the weather is not as humid as I thought it would be. It is especially hot when we walk home from school at noon. Another nice thing about Ghana is the many different sports played here. One of the best things is the beach. We have made many friends both white and black."

Us too. The professionals, business and artistic people we began to know were warm and welcoming. One pleasant feature was dance parties. Despite the heat, the women sure taught us how to shake our behinds.

"Shake your booty" became routine once we started to get better at it. Not what I was taught in my middle school dancing class by a long shot. Amazing that despite that constant activity most people, particularly women, displayed substantial girth.

Speaking of women, they were securely in charge. In the market the mammys ruled the roost. Goods were spread out on cloths on the ground, with piles of spices adding color and scent. The most appealing place in the market was the section selling "mammy cloth." The colorful cotton was largely imported from Java (Indonesia) and other sources. Women were swathed in long lengths of cloth wrapped around their bodies, with pouches for babies in the front. (Some carried babies tightly strapped to a board on their backs.) The designs have traveled the world in intervening years and perhaps been slightly tamed. They were wild and wonderful. I bought a lot of mammy cloth, for tablecloths and for clothes. I was very grateful for my sewing machine because I soon realized I had to change up to three times a day, and the simple sheath dress was a staple. Using the wild designs was a creative challenge.

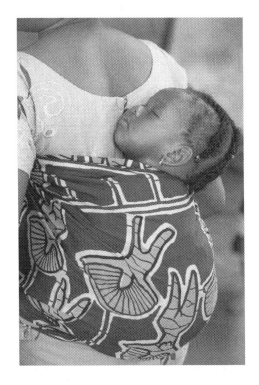

One Christmas I purchased a mammy cloth pattern in the market and asked a seamstress-friend to make us matching bathrobes. Buying matching bathrobes for his family had been a tradition of my father's, and the urge made me a bit nostalgic.

I mentioned one day that I wished I had had my ears pierced to enjoy a pair of fancy earrings I had purchased on a trip to Abidjan (in the nearby Ivory Coast.) Our prominent judge friend told me his "Auntie Martha" performed this deed "professionally" somewhere out in the bush. We got the directions, and proceeded to go and see her. Gordon wrote Dick:

"We went to see a little old native lady to have this done and I'm afraid that pretty soon your mother will have a couple of those attractive drooping ear lobes like the Masai women which you can stick a basketball through." No such problem, just that they were a little uneven. What could you expect from a hot needle plunged through an ear lobe into a piece of ice, nowhere near a ruler? Almost perfect job, no infection.

The beach scene was indeed spectacular. Ocean beaches in Accra and nearby produced strong surf and undertow. So we traveled a little out of town to a beach on a lagoon. Driving the roads in Accra required one to be alert. On the side of each street was a "*jube*," swiftly running water carrying trash and sewage. The smell of the jubes was intense. It was important not to drive too close and risk the tires falling in.

Andy described the area, "The beach is lined with small beach houses not near as big as the old one back on Lake Michigan. We got a beach house with some friends we met on the boat. The lagoon looks different every week we go. Depending on the tide, we lie down in the water and surf in or out on our backsides with our feet sticking up out of the water."

Soon, however, we were lucky to meet an Australian architect and his family, who invited us to spend Sunday at their beach hut in the other direction, a town called Ada on the Volta river. This became a blessedly regular event. We would unload our gear onto a boat which deposited us onto a spit of beach. We dove for oysters, ate, drank (a lot), waterskied, drank more, napped a little, and eventually toasted and happy, drove back to Accra. Our kids and their kids were exactly the same age and became fast friends. One Sunday they roasted a large barracuda in a pit in the sand. Learn something new every day!

Having Dick away required quite a lot of updates to him. A number of trips to the cities and villages nearby gave us the ingredients. Gordon wrote a lengthy account which I quote practically in its entirety:

"I was to represent the Ambassador at the traditional yam festival at Asankgrawa. I made a speech which had to be translated into *Twi*, (pronounced 'tree,') the language of the Ashanti tribe. I gave the principal chief some medicine to worm the village, a selection of books for the local secondary school, and 75 cutlasses. The latter is a kind of machete used for all sorts of farm work. They have probably put the damned things to use by now and wiped out the next village.

'The highpoint of the almost endless festivities was purification of the stool. The stool, to the tribes of Ghana, is just that, a stool, a piece of furniture. It is believed to contain the spirit of the tribe. They brought out their ancient stool, black as pitch. I had given them a bottle of gin and a bottle of Scotch to use for the ceremony, called "pouring the libation." They sip some and pour some (Beefeaters, no less) on the ground to pacify their ancestors. Then they brought in a sheep which didn't much want to participate, and was turned over to the executioner after being twirled over head several times. The jugular was severed, and the important part, the blood, quickly collected, was worked into the stool until it took on a crimson hue. Then they broke up some boiled eggs and scattered the pieces along with mashed yams all over the stool. A relative of the sheep was cut up and chunks of meat were scattered around the stool. Everybody around seemed to think it was stupendous, so who was I to knock it? They treated me wonderfully, because I had supplied the gin."

The next ceremony which featured Gordo (and more gin) among the celebrities was called an "outdooring." The custom originated with the Ga, another of the local tribes. A young man with whom Gordon had worked came to see him a few days after the birth of his new son, and asked Gordo if he would "outdoor" the baby. Quickly accepting, as a distinct honor, he took Joe out to lunch to get briefed as to exactly what he would have to do,

"Saturday morning," I reported home, "When the alarm buzzed shortly after four, we set out for Joe's house (a city-dwelling Ga) in the still full moon. Quite a crowd was assembled on the doorstep, including venerable elders who were notably anxious to see what sort of liquid we'd brought along as libation. Joe handed Gordon a tin of talcum powder and directed him to outline a circle about a yard in diameter in front of the house on the freshly swept earth. A woman then emerged from the house and swiftly handed Gordon a tiny, stark-naked, seven day old infant and the outdooring was under way.

The baby was placed down on the dirt in the circle and an unshod Gordo stepped over him three times, nudged him three times with his toe, and then raised him three times to the moon, all the while lecturing to the remarkably oblivious fellow that he was to grow up in emulation of his worthy elders and follow in the footsteps of his illustrious godfather, who then proclaimed him Hans Gordon Kwame Addortey Addo. The ceremony was thus ended and everyone settled down to the serious business of passing the hat, the baby's uncle goes to each guest and receives a few shillings or crumpled notes. The assembled throng chants a Ga "thank you" and toasts the wee one with an unpalatable corn brew called '*meda*,' and then in turn with beer, schnapps, and Scotch. The baby was thoroughly toasted, and all before 6 a.m. By this time the old codgers and Gordon had sworn eternal love, and the former had requested about seven scholarships."

I cannot put off any longer the discussion about the local food. While we cooked western style at home, when entertained we often needed to partake in the national food, called "*kenkey fufu*". The basis is a pounded yam with a stew on top. The yam is unlike the one which is familiar in the states, it is white, utterly tasteless, and heavy as lead. In the market you could purchase the meat ingredient including bush rat. (That is what all the beautiful spices were intended to enliven.) When we went to Ghanaian dinner parties, which was often, the hostess usually served western food alongside the *kenkey fufu*. But if you partook of food in the rural areas that's all you got. The Ghanaians couldn't get enough of it. In contrast, also popular and *beautifully* prepared, often served at midday parties, were curries. Rice was plentiful, the basis for chicken or seafood, served with "small chop:" accompanying the curry were little dishes of chopped cocoanut, ground nuts (we know them as peanuts), tomatoes, raisins, hard boiled egg, onions and chutney. This we could have enjoyed every day of the week.

The yearning for more of the fresh foods we cherished and missed was part of the motivation for frequent trips across the neighboring country of Dahomey into Togo, which had been under French control. Lomē, was a dusty village with three French delicatessens. Crossing borders with diplomatic license plates made it possible to pass without undue delay; the guards were concerned with a lot of smuggling, both of cocoa going out and of arms in, the effort of the deposed president seeking to rally support and reinstate his regime. The delis stocked *pain de mie*, or rye bread, unavailable in Accra. Also the unheard of delicacy, celery. French goods arrived several times a week. We carefully timed our visits – the trip took about two hours.

The pace of life in Accra perfectly matched the temperature. It made no sense to try and charge around at the usual pace. Everywhere I looked there was a body stretched out, or crumpled up, sound asleep. Turn your back, and there was kuku, dozing in the kitchen chair. Between courses Robert, the steward, napped on the kitchen step. Laborers always went to work with a small boy at their heels, who did the actual work while the guy getting paid took a snooze. It wasn't the people, it was the tropics, and it was really very pleasant once you came to grips with the necessities of existence. Sprawled in the living room, eyes fixed on the shiny blades of the undulating, rhythmic, improperly hung ceiling fan revolving endlessly above, transporting me into the never-never, - well what the hell – I felt like I was smack in the mainstream, doing just what everybody was doing in New York, only my LSD was electrical.

One day I was stuck in traffic watching the end of Ramadan being noisily celebrated by parades, drums and dancing. Muhammed never in his wildest dreams could have imagined what the Africans had done with his religion of duty and austerity! I soon learned that one needed always to stay alert in Ghana traffic. It was so

hot the car windows were always open. I felt a tapping
on my left elbow and naturally turned to see what it was
about. Instinct told me to quickly look to the right, there
was a stick studded with razor blades reaching in to grab
my purse on the passenger seat. Fortunately one loud yell
and the would-be robber disappeared. Purses henceforth
were stashed beneath my seat.

A classic brush with the outside world involved
the official visit of a prominent administration official,
(Nicholas Katzenbach) and his wife, Lydia. They were
well programmed and got the kind of picture of Ghana
and our involvement there that they wanted, through
intensive discussions with government leaders and a
few key visits there. I was detailed take charge of the
Mrs. Katzenbach's itinerary. My first impression as they
deplaned was that I was in for a dour few days, but they
began to melt (literally and figuratively) and I realized I
had an extraordinarily receptive and responsive woman
on my hands and it became a huge pleasure. Our rounds
included the market, the museum, a climb to a roof for
an incredible view into a lorry park that isn't a typical
tourist attraction but typifies the industry of West
Africa. Plus a visit to the maternity clinic of one of the
hospitals, a luncheon with some of Accra's leading lights
in social welfare and education, a trip into the country
to visit a sculptor at his studio home, and in the evening
a dinner and dance performance at the university. I
wondered at how they could keep up that kind of pace
throughout their reconnaissance trip but was gratified at

their apparent appreciation. Visitors came often, official or no, requiring some of the same treatment.

There was one endeavor with local people I especially enjoyed. I finally convinced the Social Welfare department that despite being an American my educational level was beyond the sixth grade, and they "let" me start to teach basic literacy to messenger/ maintenance types in the local tobacco company, men who had never been to school. (The Department was concerned about my accent, so I affected British a little.) I had a wonderful time with those eight to ten gentlemen who came to class twice a week. We made great progress, although I totally failed to get them to correctly pronounce the word "the."

Our young Andy got it into his head (we never knew what was in there) to get himself a pet snake. I do not recall where he got the young, three foot python, but do recall insisting it stay in a sturdy cage in Andy's room. It got fed a mouse or a gerbil once a week. One night it came in handy. Ghanaians invited to dinner never wanted to go home, long after the hosts were ready to call it a night. I invented a trick and went to get the snake (I do not remember if Andy had named it) to wrap around my neck. It was quite cool and not a bit slimy. The guests were unnerved, and went home. "We are Africans, "they protested on the way to their cars. When we went home a couple of years later Andy transported the creature in his airline bag which he tried surreptitiously to unzip

during the flight in order to check on its wellbeing.
Believe me I sat next to him the whole time and never
sneaked a nap.

A year into our stay we had a sad family item
to deal with, a message of my father's death in
Arizona after a night out at the opera following a day
transplanting *Phoenix Roebelini* on his ranch. Not a bad
way for a good man to exit, if he had to. I flew to Chicago
and on to Phoenix to be with my mother. She was strong,
and agreed to travel out to spend the next Christmas
with us in Accra. I knew she would.

Her trip proved to be a great joy. She came out
on some sort of a paqueboat, We took her of course
over to Dahomey to see the village on stilts and to Lomē
on the way home. She endeared herself to Ghanaians
and everybody else. Robert and Philippe were crushed
when she had to go home. But when she left we knew we
were heading for a wind-down of Ghana even though we
didn't know then what was coming next. There was the
tantalizing possibility (especially for mother) of a posting
at home.

Our summer holiday trip took us to Morocco,
where we had heard about the American School of
Tangier. Andy had aged out of Ghana schools whereas
Billy would enter a new American school comprising
only middle school grades. I had taken the advice of
my landlord/doctor and decided to travel to Frankfurt
for a hysterectomy. Following non eventful surgery I
stayed in the flat of a colleague in Frankfurt, and took
advantage of an offer to take a night train to Berlin
across the Soviet sector. That went off without incident,
particularly as we had arranged for Andy to visit for the
month of July with a Swiss family for total immersion in
French. The Geslains learned a lot of English. M. Geslain
took Andy to hunt truffles in the mountains, among other
delights such as the French food, about which he raved.
When the time came for him to leave, Andy met me in
Geneva after my brief recovery, and we then traveled
to Madrid to meet Gordon and Billy who came up from
Accra via Mallorca, and Dick who came from the states

where he had spent the early summer with cousins and grandmother, including a trip to Bermuda. The hotel staff thought the meeting of the five from almost four corners of the world was very amusing. Andy was stuck by a dour mood in Geneva, a dark pall in the minds of everybody we encountered which was the product of Soviet tanks rolling through Prague, next door. Wikipedia recounts the events thus:

"Soviet leaders were concerned over these recent developments (the "Prague Spring") in Czechoslovakia. Recalling the 1956 uprising in Hungary, leaders in Moscow worried that if Czechoslovakia carried reforms too far, other satellite states in Eastern Europe might follow, leading to a widespread rebellion against Moscow's leadership of the Eastern Bloc. There was also a danger that the Soviet Republics in the East, such as the Ukraine, Lithuania, Latvia, and Estonia might make their own demands for more liberal policies. After much debate, the Communist Party leadership in Moscow decided to intervene to establish a more conservative and pro-Soviet government in Prague."

Political comment: Does this sound familiar? ("*Plus ca change, plus c'est la mème chose.*")

From Madrid we traveled across the straits to the coast of Morocco. The school in Tangier was small, very demanding, a shot in the dark. We hoped beyond hope that Andy would rise to the challenge. After visiting the school we headed across Morocco as a family to see the snake charmers in the D'jma el Fna in Fez, the glorious markets of Rabat, the snow in the Atlas mountains. Dick left us and flew back to Rome, we left Andy back in Tangier with our fingers crossed, and headed back to Accra.

The next Christmas vacation brought us all together with affection obvious among the boys, not long enough to fight. They appeared to have outgrown that childish and adolescent condition anyway.

It was decided that Andy would stay at home after vacation. Nevertheless his feelings about the venture in Tangier were moving:

"I was absolutely fascinated with the place every day I was there, with every glance into the diverse cultures, the distinct French, Spanish and Arabic presence in the city, every turn of my head leading to a new experience."

Andy spent the next four months in Accra doing various jobs at his father's office, studying a bit of French, swimming and playing tennis. In short order the time came for us to bring the Ghana years to an end. We had made an enormous number of close friends; the party to celebrate our departure was a swinger to end all swingers. One of my acquaintances, not a favorite by a long shot, asked me the next day if she could please have my guest list. I impolitely declined and told her to do her own fishing.

We left Accra without Billy, whose school was to continue for a month. Gordon had gone to Paris for a meeting. Bill stayed with friends who already had five children, one his best friend. I traveled on the plane along with Andy and his snake, to meet my mother in New York ("please get us a reservation at a hotel which takes snakes.")

Chapter Three

DC Interim

The family reunited in Washington where we needed to look for a house, having happily been assigned to a posting at home. While we were looking we stayed with my sister, Bibsie, and her husband on the top floor of their large house in Cleveland Park where the snake got loose, ending that phase of life. (Its reappearance in Sam's underwear drawer helped to end their marriage.)

Dickie had become Richard by that time, by unilateral decree, and he decided to come home and finish secondary school in Washington. Bill went to a local junior high, and Andy to a tightly supervised school called Emerson Institute where he could work to get his GED. We were delighted at Richard's admission to Dartmouth, from whence his father had graduated. I went to work in a Public Relations firm while Gordon traveled constantly to Africa on inspection visits. I stopped every day in a health club where I learned Pilates. I decided it was about time to learn how to use a computer so I rented a funny shaped portable called Osborne to work through the initial stages. It soon became obvious that I could never learn Wordstar, an IBM based program which had command lines that looked to me like mathematical formulas (never my strength.) So I bought an Apple Macintosh, and a new love affair began, one which has never ended.

I soon volunteered at a unique employment office with the understanding that if the right sounding job came across my horizon I could apply. One soon did. I started working (for pennies) for the National Welfare Rights Organization, a group high on the civil rights spectrum, for a dynamic former chemist named George Wiley and his covey of welfare mothers from whom I began learning how the other half struggles to live halfway decent lives. This education and the women who provided it have stayed in my mind and heart to this day. One of the chief delights was in finding that I (we) were on the Nixon Enemies List. I understand that it was well known at the State Department. It is an enormous tribute to Gordon's progressive political attitude that he did not stew over any potential effect on his government career. (He was working, after all, for the organization that had once been headed by Edward R. Murrow, who made the famous declaration against Senator Joe McCarthy.)

One particularly memorable occasion with NWRO was the meeting we had in the offices of Elliot

Richardson at the Department of Health and Human Services. There we sat: George, at least twelve of the welfare mothers, and I, arguing across the table with a bevy of bureaucrats about the level of the poverty line. $5500 was the annual level we were volubly fighting for at the time. We obtained few of the objectives but certainly made enough impression to become recognized as a viable voice in the dialogue. DC press usually appeared at George's press conferences and provided welcome visibility.

The kids were growing up. With a working mother they learned to cope with such daily requirements as their laundry; I gave each one a laundry hamper, showed them how to use the washer/dryer, and launched them on their own. Color separation was not part of the lesson. Neither was matching socks. I did manage to meet them for dinner every evening at our kitchen table, with one of their friends asking incredulously: "Do you do this every night?" Gordon was away a great deal, inspecting posts in Africa, averaging two weeks every month leaving me a "single mother." Dinner was obligatory nevertheless.

Eventually, after about three years, the prospect of a new post arrived. There was going to be an opening in Iran. We were intrigued at the thought of such a prodigious change of scenery and culture. The area of the Middle East was more fraught with conflict than ever.

The Christmas before we were due to leave
we made a spur of the moment decision to try for a
Caribbean vacation "on the cheap." An agent told us about
a hotel on the island of St. Maarten, but there were no
flights available. When she called with an urgent last
minute availability we jumped at the chance to go to
Marigot. It was terrific. Among the little hotel's charms
was a swimming pool with stools at one end where one
could swim up for a drink at the pool bar. We made a
Christmas tree out of a single twelve inch pine branch
studded with marshmallows and hoped our tradition of
being "*en famille*" at Christmas would never be broached.

Rich was at college, Bill was fifteen, Andy was
trying to deal with school, I was at work. And the posting
was announced.

I realized I needed to go to Tehran in the
middle of the year. Gordon had to precede me and left
in April of 1973. Andrew, attending the art school at
the Corcoran Gallery of Art, rented a small basement
apartment with a friend. What about Billy? No problem,
he got in touch with the hotel in St. Maarten and got
a job as a bartender in the pool. Novel idea, a good
solution for the month or so from when school ended in
Washington and before the opening of school in a brand
new place.

Chapter Four

Four and a Half Years in Iran

Preparation for the new posting involved renting our house and preparing a wardrobe. Why was this an issue? Hard to believe, but the wife of Gordon's predecessor in the Tehran job called and asked me if she could come and take a look in my closet. Somewhat taken aback, I got the point. The social scene in Tehran was very formal; evening clothes were absolutely necessary. Nothing like a challenge! I loaded up with a few long dresses as well as a group of books from the Foreign Service Institute to help me learn Farsi, a higher priority.

We had a lot to learn. Persian culture was born sixteen centuries before the birth of Christ, sixteen hundred and fifty years before the birth of Mohammed and Islam, suffused the modern society, and was (and is) revered by everyone in the current era. We looked forward to seeing the famous miniatures dating from the Achmaenedid Empire, the stately ruins of Persepolis, the famous gardens, customs, celebrations, the growing wealth of Iranian film, and sumptuous food. Will Durant, an American writer of history, stated in a 1948 address to the Iran American society that "For thousands of years Persians have been creating beauty." A lot to look forward to.

Gordon had to get to the new post a couple of months before I was free to travel. House and kids' arrangements took precedence. Bill was out in the Caribbean in his bartending job and would join us in Tehran in short order.

Gordo met me at the airport in Tehran and told me we were going directly to the bazaar. I was certainly diving right in to the new assignment! He and Dakhil, his driver, told me there was a drink to try in the bazaar that I was going to love. "Couldn't it wait?" I wondered. No, had to try "*doogh*" right away. They were right, I loved it (yoghurt and soda water and a sprig of mint) and was astounded with the bazaar. Unlike most other outdoor markets, enormous (virtually miles in size.) The Tehran bazaar featured goods for every need: skinned animals hanging on racks, acres of gold jewelry, clothing, household goods in abundance, and carpets, carpets, carpets. I was determined to spend quite a lot of time down there but I wanted to go see my house.

Waiting for me were Amir, the cook, and Abbas, the yard man. I grew to love Abbas, and tolerate Amir.

The house had certain charm but needed work. Nicest
aspect of it was the pool underneath the cantilevered
deck over the garden. The living room had a bed for Amir
at one end, which we clearly needed to remove. I got
the embassy to cover the walls and ceiling of the small
powder room with orange paper. It looked great and got
a lot of compliments. Too bad the landlord decided to sell
the house shortly after our arrival.

No matter. Have I mentioned that by now I had
earned a PhD in moving? What we found on the other side
of town was very satisfactory. Tehran was not beautiful,
by a long shot, but the residential areas were shaded
with big, old trees, every property had tall walls. Our
garden was sizeable, suitable for entertaining, very nice.
The principal streets were wide, particularly in the north
end of the city where we lived. Downtown (bazaar and
environs) was a different story.

Abbas brought to our attention a custom far
from our imagination. A major holiday in Iran was
the celebration of *Ashura* which commemorated-
the martyrdom of the Prophet Muhammad's grandson,
Hussein ibn Ali, in 680 A.D. Shiite Muslims observe
Ashura through mourning rituals such as self flagellation
and reenactments of the martyrdom. After hours walking
the streets flinging chains on his back poor bloody Abbas
would return for a rest.

A major feature of living in Iran was and remains the traffic! No number of exclamation points could possibly describe adequately what went on in those streets. Picture a four lane road, with six lanes of cars so close together you could be in trouble if you took a deep breath. Drivers regularly lost their tempers and socked the adjoining car as it went by. Traffic jams were endemic, of course. Motorcycles and scooters wound through the lanes. Inevitably somebody got out of his car to try and unjumble the messes. I soon learned that the most appropriate word for Tehran traffic was "*sholuq*" which you translate by intertwining your fingers and writhing them over and under. People walking and crossing in the streets followed an age old custom. If you don't see somebody he isn't there, so they never looked.

Most women wore *chador* (full length black robe) outside of their homes, in the street, in shops. The veil had been outlawed by the father of the Shah, but only the educated, upper classes dismissed it entirely. It produced a certain comfort; although it was not decreed in the Koran that women must completely cover themselves, the men demanded it. It was unseemly that their women should be seen by men not their husbands. Young girls always had to have a male relative if not their parents accompany them away from home. The sneaking peeks between the boys and the girls were only just coming on the scene. At the university the standards were less stringent. A number of young women wore only a head-scarf. I had a few experiences in which I needed to put on the chador. This was the case in Isfahan and Mashad, in order to enter the mosque. I felt completely claustrophobic, and couldn't stand it. In Mashad I apparently left traces of the lipstick I wiped off, and heard angry hissing around me. Dakhil fortunately whisked me to the door and remembered where we had left our shoes.

The chador clad women's anonymity saved them from exhibiting any manners, at least manners as I had been accustomed to them in other societies. Women aggressively pushed and nudged others out of their way, when shopping in the bazaar or in shops. It became very annoying. One day intent on purchasing some sewing supplies I got totally fed up and tapped a pusher where I presumed her shoulder was. "*Nobate man ast*", said I firmly. She looked at me surprised and stepped aside. I had informed her that it was "my turn".

Iranian food was certainly one of the highlights of our stay in the country (and we continue to seek it out back at home.) Glorious fruits eaten alone or as flavors in meat dishes. Kebab is the best known, served with rice ("*chelo-kebab*") whole onions, tomatoes, an enormous variety. It could be beef or chicken. Greens and yoghurt accompany every meal. The bread came in several permutations and was uniformly marvelous. When Gordon and I took walks around our neighborhood on Sunday mornings we always bought "*barbari*" coming fresh out of the ovens on flat paddles. Trouble was, we always ate it before we could get it home. The even flatter bread, called "*lavash*," has made it to Western markets and is a familiar item today.

Iran society was very stratified, virtually from south to north. The country had grown prosperous since the 1974 gasoline crisis began; the gross national product grew from approximately two billion a year to twenty two billion. The business class became enormously wealthy, and it showed. Believe me, it showed. (Refer to my comment about my closet.) Wealthy women routinely flew to Paris on weekends to shop at Dior. There was an International Women's Club which I was invited to join in view of Gordon's position at the Embassy. I politely declined protesting that I didn't have an afternoon mink. Besides, I was busy in the afternoons. Explanation follows a little later.

The wealth came from the rise in the international price of oil. Modern Iranian society emerged when the Shah began to emphasize education, land reform, and health care. The Shah had been recalled from exile and placed in his position following a nasty coup engineered, it is rightfully claimed, by American and British anger at the nationalization of Iranian oil. Prior to nationalization in 1956 oil had been managed by the British who extracted the lion's share of the revenues. The Anglo American Oil Company was abruptly renamed the National Iranian Oil Company by an elected Prime Minister, Mohammed Mossadegh. Mossadegh was overthrown by the American CIA working with British interests, and the Shah installed as head of government. His modernizing evolution masked a growing autocratic style which angered the merchants of the bazaar as well as the all important mullahs and the students. The merchant class largely kept their heads in the sand as business opportunities skyrocketed, but symptoms were everywhere but not evident – at least to the foreign diplomats and businessmen coming into the country in droves to take advantage of the new prosperity. The autocracy brooked no dissent, no opposition parties, a pervasive secret police presence (known as *Savak*), arrested students, suspicion and conspiracy theories were everywhere. Guests in our home often scanned the light fixtures for signs of listening devices and stopped talking when the cook walked into the room.

The Iran-American Society (*the Anjoman*) was an important institution in Tehran, run by a board headed by a prominent ophthalmologist. It occupied a handsome multipurpose building in the north of Tehran, and in branches in smaller cities. Its mission was to teach English (to about 25,000 students a year), bring American cultural events to the country, run a well organized and intensely popular library, and incidentally to provide classes in Farsi to foreign personnel in the city. It did not take me long to enroll. In the four years I lived in Iran there were few vacations from class; I found learning Farsi a true window vastly improving my enjoyment of daily life and my ability to deal with my tea boys (see discussion about my office) and difficult strangers in the markets.

The closest new friend by far was a young woman who taught at the university, Fera began immediately helping with my understanding of the way things worked. My "eyes and ears." She was a frequent guest in our house and we spent a lot of time in the bazaar, even in the dead of winter in a coffee house called the *"Aban bar"* where we sat propped on cushions with our feet under a low table covered in carpets and warmed by a heater underneath. Our affectionate friendship included travel together and has thrived to this day. We took several memorable trips. The first one was to Alamut. a magnificent castle in the Alamut Valley built on top of a high rock. The rock is 200 m high and covers an area of over 40 acres. With its steep slope and deep and dangerous ravine, the rock looked practically inaccessible, forming a part of the fort's structure. Only ruins of the fort and some towers were apparent. But the trip was known to be an adventure, we got a group of friends (and Andy, "home" on holiday) and with hare-brained courage set out to conquer it. We pitched tents in the valley and proceed to climb the next day. It was endless. Towards the eighth hour we spied a broken down lorry running along and through the river and climbed aboard. There weren't many floorboards but we couldn't have cared less. We called it the *"shotor khan"* (camel) express.

I will describe the most memorable trip
with my friend Fera a little later. One of Gordon's
Washington colleagues suggested we should augment our
understanding of the Middle East by taking a trip across
the gulf. The Persian Gulf, you have to understand, not
the Arabian Gulf. Augment we did, starting in Bahrain,
down through Oman, Qatar, and to Saudi Arabia. What
a learning experience that was! In Saudi my hostess,
the wife of the Consul General, took me immediately
to the market to have a long sleeved and floor length
garment made. When in Rome, etc..... I was astounded and
disgusted learning that Saudi women were forbidden to
drive cars. I was informed that we were to attend a tea
party that afternoon. I tried protesting that tea parties
were "not my thing." "Come," she wisely persisted, and
it was indeed one of the most unusual events I had ever
attended: as soon as the guests were inside the long
robes came off displaying sexy garments and the dancing
began.

Another revelation was the solution to the no-
spirits problem facing the expatriate community. Half of
the houses rented to Americans had stills in their extra
bathrooms where they brewed their own. No challenge
whatsoever to Chivas Regal.

Then my twin sister Judy arrived for a visit, at
the end of which we took off for a trip to Israel. It was
1974, just after the end of the only war in which the
Israelis suffered defeat. The morale was dismal. We

visited my former professor in Ethiopia and got an earful. We traveled down country on a tourist bus. The driver pointed out a dome in the distance (Dimona, the Israili nuclear facility), and described it to the passengers as a shoe factory. Not many of them appeared to question that assertion.

Plenty of activity, yet something was missing. Billy was in the International school downtown, Andy and Richard were in the States respectively in art school and college, there were no important family demands on my time and there appeared to be a larger need outside. It was shocking and depressing to hear stories of personnel being hired to come and work in the country with no preparation to understand the culture and/or the language. A prescription for disaster. I talked to an American friend who had been in the country for many years (married to an Iranian woman), we decided to form a company to provide orientation services to the ever increasing U.S. and other nationals rapidly arriving. We soon had a cynical awakening: the business executives didn't have as much concern over their employees' needs as they did for their own. Consider an executive arriving in a country as foreign to them as Iran, presented with no way to get the day-to-day problems solved. There was not even an English language telephone book. And so Executive Services Company was born.

This opportunity was just lying there on the floor waiting for somebody to pick it up and run. A basic tenet in building a business, I was learning, was to find and capitalize upon a need. A lot more productive than the American habit of promoting needs and supporting the advertising industry to convince the public it had them.

Of course I had to go and get permission for such a drastic operation from the American Ambassador. He was firm: Keep your head down. "If you get into any trouble we don't know you." His embassy was being overrun by business executives from the States who were asking for logistical help – and it seemed there was a solution in view. The Ambassador was Richard Helms. former director of the CIA. He and his lovely wife, Cynthia, became great supporters and even greater friends.

I rented an office in a building across the street from a leading hotel and employed a young American wife of an Iranian as a secretary. It didn't take long for word to get around that "that business across the street from the Intercontinental can help you." We grew. To an entire floor, to two floors, with a staff of American and British women, a Persian translator on call, and a young Armenian girl, just as interested as I in purposeful work.

Clients came from around the world. U.S. engineering and oil companies, the Australian Meat Board, Danish and Japanese companies, all in search of space to work, staff to help. I went to visit the Dean of the Harvard-led business school to discuss a fundamental problem. "How do you charge for services, Barkev?" I asked. "Peggy," he said seriously, "There are two essential ways you make this decision. 'Cost plus', or 'what the traffic will bear'. Which do you think is applicable here?" First lesson of my pre-business school education.

Communication was the major problem. In the days before the Internet, telex ruled. In Tehran at the time there were 600 telex lines, 400 of which were owned by the military. The remaining lines groaned with over-activity and demands. There was an American company in the next building which had one; for a sizeable consideration to its manager we strung a line across the roof and lo and behold had telex access. A wonderful older gentleman named Aram (uncle of Claudine, my Armenian assistant) came every night from his day job to send telexes down country and across the oceans. In the morning reams of paper from the machine covered our floor and needed to be sorted and read by phone to recipients, delivery was out of the question. (Remember traffic?) The reams of paper were in three copies, one for the client, one for us, and the imperative third for Savak. We had to send them their copies regularly.

The phone system was barely better, Neither was the power supply. We had ten electric typewriters and one manual, which went into major production when the power went down. I employed two Iranian "tea boys" whom I called the "magic fingers". Much of their time, when they weren't bringing little cups of tea to my clients in the office, was spent dialing the telephone to try and get calls through. They also had to take letters to the Post Office every day – until one day I found a cache of un-mailed letters months old for which the tea boys had collected for postage.

Clear but small time evidence of the endemic problem of corruption was mail delivery: my mailman came one day and asked for his "*mahjuneh*," his monthly bribe. I protested, saying he already had a salary. "Do you want your mail or not?," he asked. My naivetē evaporated. The subject of "considerations" for access was in full view. It was said that one of the beneficiaries was the sister of the Shah. I told clients without hesitation that they would inevitably be confronted with the five percent.

The company grew beyond my foolish expectations, produced an invaluable service, and thankfully everybody involved had a great time. Clients were happy, wonderful staff too, And the Embassy commercial office was relieved of the myriad problems they did not have the capacity to tackle. I was busy and gratified. At one point we landed a contract for the administration of Iran staff of a major firm, beating out one of the major U.S. companies vying for the job.

Early on a scruffy Persian appeared in the office carrying what looked like an old medical bag. Behrooz opened it and showed me a heap of somewhat rusty tins of Caspian Sea caviar. Thus began a regular habit of obtaining the black gold for clients and myself. When Behrooz showed up I would buy a tin and call Amir. "I'm bringing dinner home. Please put chopped onions, hard-boiled eggs and capers in the fridge and go home. No need to wait." We suspected that this cache was "poached", meaning not obtained legally from the Caviar fishery up on the Caspian Sea. It was especially wonderful and one third the price of official supplies. Iranian customs were becoming mine.

At dinner parties (not at our house) there were mounds of caviar on the buffet tables. One party in particular occurred during the visit of Henry Kissinger, accompanied by scads of press, at the home of the Prime Minister. These eminent and sophisticated reporters whispered to Gordon,"How do we eat it?" The answer was: "Don't wait, get in there and fill your plate."

The parties, as I inferred earlier, were continuous, and gorgeous. We would often enter the garden of the host and hostess to find tables scattered upon Persian rugs, with glittering lights strung in the trees. We soon had really close friends among the Persian society, academics and businessmen. (I usually handed out my business card to the latter, word was getting around about the company.) The food was invariably sumptuous and delicious. We also entertained frequently on a less glamorous scale. Perhaps three or four tables of six or eight. Amir was up to the job, and hired the servers needed from the Embassy motor pool, they all knew the drill, the dress requirements, and usually what the guests wanted to drink. Gordon's social secretary took care of the seating arrangements. I would come home from the office and ask Amir what I could do to help. "Just fix the flowers, and go take a nap," he'd say. I didn't protest. You can get spoiled living like that.

There were clearly tensions in the room, in town, in restaurants, at the university. In was inevitable that trouble was brewing but there was no clear intelligence about its source. The main reason nobody admittedly envisioned the fact that it was coming from the bazaar was that nobody in the Embassy, with the exception of one junior officer, knew enough Farsi to sniff out the problem. I had started studying at the *Anjoman* right after we arrived, and probably got to about third grade. It was enormously helpful for social and listening purposes and Iranians really appreciated when foreigners made the effort. I never acquired any competence in reading or writing. The script is read from right to left, with practically no space between words. We studied beautifully illustrated children's picture books to begin learning to read.

Living the Tehran life, one of the greatest enjoyments was studying and buying carpets. I observed at one of the first dinners in a Persian home, that the room was covered with large and small carpets of varying design and color, no two alike. They almost overlapped, producing a dignified riot of color. We began to visit

the carpet shops, usually on Friday mornings. That was
the Sabbath, of course, however many of the carpet
merchants were Jewish. They covered their windows
with paper and welcomed viewers in for lessons and to
buy. Most often we sat high up upon mounds of carpets
around the showroom (drinking tea) while the owner
described the provenance of the rug spread out on top
of the growing pile in the center of the room. People
were encouraged to take home whatever they wished
to consider buying. You would leave your name with the
owner (who knew you pretty well in short order) and
return later either with a check or a reject. We kidded
that we were going to stay in Iran until the carpets
on the floor began to overlap. One truly becomes fond
of one's carpets, it is a strange bond. To this day I
remember where all of the carpets came from and the
memories flood in.

Mention of the Sabbath also brings me to the
subject of skiing. Tehran's altitude at the base of the
Alborz mountains was about 7500 feet, top of the highest
ski lift at the ski resort of Dizine was about 11,400 feet.
We would drive from our house for an hour and a half
and park almost at the top. Then sling our backpacks on
our shoulders and ski down to leave them on a restaurant
terrace. We would invariably go on Sundays, a work day
in Iran. (Executive Services' boss took the day off.)
The area was jammed on Fridays, but the expatriate
community and the Shah and the Queen skied Sundays.
The resort area had surface lifts, chair lifts and gondolas,
two or three restaurants. It was absolutely delightful

Photo of Mohammed Reza Pahlavi, Shah of Iran, and his wife, Empress Farah, wave goodbye prior to boarding an aircraft after a visit to the United States by SSZ in public domain. IMAGE SOURCE: http://en.wikipedia.org/wiki/File:Mohammed Reza Pahlavi and his wife.jpg

Winter arrived abruptly sometime in November. Snow was plentiful, a problem for the city's flat roofs. During a snowstorm the streets were filled with men yelling "*barfi*" (snow remover) waiting to be called in to climb onto the roofs and scrape the snow off. The climate the rest of the year was temperate, never too hot in the more northern parts of the city due to the altitude. Tehran has an average annual rainfall of 15 inches in northern neighborhoods, providing a fairly reliable water supply.

Of course we made numerous trips to other parts of Iran, for Gordon to visit branches of the Iran-American Society, and for the all important travels to other times and customs. Persepolis was an early target. It dates to the Achaemenid Empire (550-330 BC) – has many remaining decorated walls of palaces despite having been looted and burned by Alexander the Great. Shiraz is a city

of gardens and roses nearby. And then, Isfahan. There is
a pervasive Iranian expression: "Isfahan is half the world"
which the visitor is at pains to dispute. It was twice the
capital city of Persia, today the art and architecture rival
anything else in the world in terms of beauty and intricacy:
palaces such as the *Ali Qapu* and *Chehel Sotoun,* the *Imam
Mosque* splendid mainly for the beauty of its seven color
mosaic tiles and calligraphic inscriptions. Mosques were
everywhere, one more handsome than the one before.

The Nasr ol Molk mosque in Shiraz by <u>dynamosquito</u> from
Niort, France, under a <u>Creative Commons license</u>. IMAGE
SOURCE: http://en.wikipedia.org/wiki/File:Nasr ol Molk
mosque inside colorful.jpg

The bazaar had an entire section devoted to the dying of wool for rugs, which we visited on several occasions, always when we were there with visitors. Out in the desert to the southeast was the city of Yazd, memorable for its towers of silence. These were structures used by the Zoroastrians; to preclude the pollution of the earth, bodies of the dead were placed atop a tower, and so exposed to the sun and scavenging birds.

Tower of Silence, <u>Yazd, Iran</u> by <u>Petr Adam Dohnálek</u> under a <u>Creative Commons license</u>. IMAGE SOURCE: http://en.wikipedia.org/wiki/File:Tower of Silence (Yazd) 004.jpg

These visits to the provinces also contributed to our study of rug culture, and sometimes added to the collection at home.

At Christmas in 1975 Gordon and I took a trip to India and Nepal. Richard and some of his friends had gone earlier to scout out India and try the climb to Base Camp Everest. We couldn't find them anywhere! We were enchanted with Nepal despite the fact that it may be the filthiest place I have ever traveled. I brought home a ten inch bronze *Ganesha* which I framed, mounted on a red velvet background and hung in my office. Ganesha is the God of Removing Obstacles, the elephant with many legs. I told the clients that rubbing his nose should ensure good luck in their Iran ventures.

Our visit to India was unrealistic, it was December, and the weather was very pleasant. We had the good fortune of finding a former student at the Iran Center, a member of a film making family in Bombay (not yet Mumbai.) She and her husband, a high- ranking naval officer, invited us to their club for dinner. It was very formal, with the waiters wearing white gloves and no shoes. We stayed (as was fortunately often possible) with colleagues of Gordon's, hospitable in the extreme. At the end of that great trip we bought a couple of copper and brass lamps made from tiffin pots, invented for the servants to take lunches to their masters getting onto the trains. These were more exotic than most. We had them shipped to our address in Tehran. When they had not arrived after 11 months I gave up on ever seeing them, but on a wondrous day a year after our return the package arrived at customs. Imagine the story it could have told. These items remain my favorite appurtenances of my living room. They defy cleaning now that I live near the ocean but no mind, they have just mellowed from the day we found them in Bombay.

The last memorable trip in this Iran saga started out as an adventure of Fera's and mine. We wanted and decided to go to Afghanistan, she to find an old friend, me to add an exciting arrow to my quiver. It was the time of *NoRuz*, the most important holiday in the culture of Iran. (This means new day, or New Year and occurs at the spring equinox. The preparations take weeks, cleaning houses, gathering foods. Why western cultures persist in celebrating the birth of a new year in ice and snow when the earth is dormant I can never rationalize after seeing when it should be celebrated.) We needed to arrange transport from Tehran, made easier when two high-ranking Embassy officers and their wives expressed an interest in going along. We requisitioned a lorry from the Embassy to be picked up in Mashad after a flight there, and drove across the Afghan border from Herat. Keep in mind, these were the days before the Soviet incursion. The country appeared to be eons behind the development in Iran, and the people curious and pleasant. We drove to Kabul without incident except for the moment when I needed a pit stop. The van left me out near an "empty" field; when I dropped my trousers to take care of the need what looked like 100 men popped up with angry faces. My god, I was in a poppy field, forbidden territory.

Fera and I stayed at Green's Hotel, infamous for the quality of hashish available at the bar. I will say nothing further about that event. There was an utterly charming shopping area in Kabul known as "Chicken" Street, where artifacts and handicrafts were on display. I bought a burka refashioned as a long dinner dress, with the "eyepiece" in the front prominent upon the chest. It was lapis blue silk and was a "dinner winner" back at home accompanied with primitively designed lapis jewelry.

A Group of Women Wearing Burkas by Nitin Madhav (USAID)
in public domain. IMAGE SOURCE: http://en.wikipedia.org/
wiki/File:Group of Women Wearing Burkas.jpg

While we were in the country Fera and I explored
the possibility of going "up country" to Kunduz. We hired
a taxi whose driver insisted on the two of us sitting
in front with him, separated from about eight Afghan
men. The men were utterly mesmerized by this young
Persian woman wearing overalls, who spoke English with
the foreign lady. (Fera went to Boulder, Colorado to
university.) Our objective in Kunduz was to find the game
of *Buzkashi* in which two opposing teams of horsemen vie
to seize the carcass of a calf or a goat and drop it behind
the goal line of the opposing team. The carcass soon

becomes pieces of a carcass, the game ends when there is nothing left to hold onto. We found the friend and the game and I had my picture taken on top of a huge white horse with no bit in its mouth. No matter, it couldn't have gone anywhere, I was fortunately surrounded by a crowd of turbaned tribesmen who prevented the horse from galloping off.

One Afghan Language is a dialect of Farsi known as Dari, different, but Fera could converse and I could understand a little. We sat on the upper level of a bar the night before the game to have a chat with some of the locals. Just before we left on this trip a friend seated next to me at a dinner party in Tehran mentioned that he had to make a trip to Afghanistan. "For business or pleasure?" I asked. "Peggy", he said to me sternly, "No Iranian ever goes to Afghanistan for pleasure." I had to disagree with my friend after this thoroughly ingratiating trip. I weep for the horrors that have overtaken this hospitable and intriguing land since 1974 when I was lucky enough to be there.

When four and a half years had passed we sensed the end of our Persian life was imminent. There was great uncertainty about how we would keep connected with the good friends in Tehran. As with all foreign service posts, the good-byes were hard. Politically things were heating up to a fever pitch. Angry mobs in the streets shouted, "*Marg bar Amrika*," death to America. Their objective was to get rid of the Shah. At the office the power was down for most of every day. The clients also could see handwriting on the wall. By the time the revolution came most expatriate business had been forced close up shop and to leave Iran.

After one successor to Gordon's job at the Embassy the next one became one of the hostages when the students stormed the building and took 52 diplomats and citizens, held in captivity for 444 days. Looking at this from outside, back in the states, was anguishing.

We decided to travel home "backwards" through the Far East. Starting in Thailand we were first astounded at the traffic manners. People stopped for pedestrians. We stayed briefly in Singapore to visit colleagues of Gordon's. Richard by this time was working in Hong Kong for Hong Kong Radio and Television, living on the island of Cheung Chau and of course we had to visit. Our first trip to the area; it was a complete eye-opener, and a great joy.

We then went to Japan for two weeks of sightseeing and visiting exquisite gardens and architecture. One of the lasting impressions was the map in the Kyoto garden which pointed out the spot where we were standing as the "Now Place." It was one of the most language intensive places I had ever been; in the subway stations when you were helplessly looking at a map people would always come up and try to help. They could understand the problems but never be able to help us in English, too terrified to try. We visited a *ryokan* where I got a lesson from women in the bathhouse. I had my kimono tied the wrong way, indicating that I was a prostitute. They re-tied it.

We finished the homeward bound trip via Hawaii, where the overwhelming impression was the size of people, so enormous, especially in contrast to the petite Japanese. My mother had helped us obtain a timeshare on Maui where we began a new endeavor, diving. We took a "resort course" where after a few hours of instruction you get taken down under to about forty feet. We sensed this would be the first of many; we were clearly hooked. The corals were splendid and the fish profuse and glorious. We had no premonition that volcanic activity in the next few years would drastically impact both.

We got back to Washington and watched the Iran situation deteriorate. It was time for the next chapter.

Chapter Five

Washington Again, Santa Fe the Land of Enchantment, and the Finale

When we got back to Washington we found a house in Georgetown which was three stories tall and fourteen feet wide. When the kids saw it they knew we were sending them a message. I set out to find a job and go to school and Gordon walked across the bridge to work as Dean of Area Studies at the Foreign Service Institute.

I enrolled in a Master's Degree program in business and decided to concentrate on finance, which was my least comfortable area. I would never have succeeded in Statistics except for the help of a fellow student (a beautiful young woman half my age) I would meet before every class to get some tutoring. The experience of running Executive Services Corporation had taught me most of what I would have gotten in marketing and management classes. This was a far cry from the Harvard Business school with which I had grown familiar in Tehran, but the "professors" I was meeting came from "around the Beltway," which meant they were on-the-job executives teaching practical solutions to problems. During this time I also decided to try to pass the infamous New York Stock Exchange "Series 7" which would give me entrée to the brokerage industry. Happily I passed both.

So, the next step began. Ten years of stock exchange experience gave me a new vocabulary and expertise. I got a lot of satisfaction really feeling that I helped people, my clients were *not* in what we now call the one percent. Our social life in D.C. was drastically altered, there was time only for working and working out and going out to movies with a few close friends. I often bicycled to work and took up Pilates at a neighborhood health spa. We moved once during those ten years to a different house, sixteen feet wide this time. It had a darling garden and a workshop for Gordon, who found himself retired when the age 65 retirement mandate was reached. He had begun carving and building furniture, starting in the little house where he persisted in sanding stuff in the living room. I was overjoyed to find the workshop in the "big" house. Its only problem was the shop's location in the basement, Gordon was so obsessed with his new project that he never saw the light of day. With the exception of one unfortunate December evening when I got mugged walking home from the bus stop, the Georgetown experience was a wonderful one.

His having retired clearly had an influence on the course of our future. We contemplated resettling, and investigated the possibility of New Mexico. My mother was then living in Albuquerque with her new husband. We went to investigate and soon realized Santa Fe would be the next enchantment. Mother gave us a piece of gorgeous "investment" property on which we built a house we ended up abandoning to move into town proper, to a city house which had begun its life as an adobe shack ninety years earlier. This was the pattern of Santa Fe adobes, they grew to accommodate growing families. By the time we bought this one we knew it had wonderful bones and would become a playground par excellence. We were on a acre and a quarter, most of which I left as meadow. We tinkered and added, a loft for a second library, large doors in every room, eventually a long indoor swimming pool in its own room attached to our bedroom where we got our exercise. We hiked, we met marvelous friends.

I got a little Arab/Paso-cross mare named Niña, we found a poodle-mutt at the shelter we named Dolly. Gordon began to love cats in spite of my decided lack of enthusiasm. He volunteered at the animal shelter and became known as "The Madam of the Cat House." Naturally he kept bringing them home.

We, particularly Gordon, also became active in an organization which was a natural extension of our overseas life, the Council on International Relations. It grew from a small but dedicated group bringing lecturers and international visitors into an active membership of over 800. Gordon's contribution was invaluable, he served as its president for four years.

In 1990 we celebrated a blessed event. We went to Washington to await the birth of our grandchild, Andy and Dorothy's. At 1 a.m on November 1st Andy called saying "you have a beautiful granddaughter." I was overjoyed and told him I had had my order in for one of those. Bek has added great happiness to my life ever since.

Gordon filled the house with remarkable furniture all with a primitive look which was convenient because he never believed in plumb lines. I helped, experimenting with finishes, and the house grew on us and with us. We lived in and loved Santa Fe for almost fifteen years, longer than we had ever lived anywhere since we were married. I claimed when we lived in that house that I was through moving and they would take me out of there in a pine box. But I have moved four times since.

Regretfully, the altitude of the glorious Sangre de Christos mountains took a toll. 7000 feet in the air in Addis and Tehran had not seemed to be a problem, but now it was clear Gordon's lungs could no longer cope. So I end this saga with the need to move to sea level, He had lived some of his young years in California, so that's where we repaired and where the stories end.

We were only renters by this time. Two houses in Santa Barbara, the second to which I moved after his death, and two locations in San Diego, where I was persuaded to join oldest son Rich and first daughter in law Selby. I had not lived near any of my children in thirty years, it is wonderful, and the others show up constantly, I have the perfect pound-found poodle mutt I named Fifi. I still do Pilates although I creak and groan.

And my head feels a lot clearer now that I have let all this out.

Thanks for coming with me on my journey.

END

POST SCRIPT AND THANKS

This account has been written by an extremely lucky and grateful person. The major source of my joy is my sons and their families. They have become best friends. We miss our Pop terribly, of course, and inevitably there have been other losses, among them my parents who lived through the years we were away with nary a complaint. I wish I could have had the counsel of my English Professor twin sister Judy, and Gordo was the writer of the family. I said before the adventures related in this book, that I was determined to "raise my sons to go." That same sister later remarked that they were "monuments to the benefit of neglect." Knock it off, Jude, the neglect hasn't hurt, they have grown up to be marvelous men, and they keep hanging around. I know you know it, even though you aren't with us to see.

How lucky can you get?

I owe great thanks to three inspirational author friends, Marjorie Hart, Don McEvoy, and Connie Burnside. The first two strong-armed me into writing this book,

Connie has been a counselor par excellence. My wizard daughter in law Selby has helped me with technical glitches. Fera Simone has been my invaluable language consultant. My sons keep remembering little episodes that shouldn't be left out, (I do too), some of them have made it to publication. Of course I have had to leave out myriad details of the boys' adventures, so I urge them to write their own books.

I hope it doesn't take them 85 years!

I direct any interested family, friends and readers to my website: **www.iampwink.com**, for some peeks into the first and last thirds of my life, and to my blog: **Peggy's Blog**, to take up where I left off. I have shrunk my first name to the one everybody knows.

Of course I missed a lot of details and maybe made a lot of mistakes. Post to the blog and get published.